Creating
Breakthrough Innovations

The Results-Driven Manager Series

The Results-Driven Manager series collects timely articles from *Harvard Management Update, Harvard Management Communication Letter,* and the *Balanced Scorecard Report* to help senior to middle managers sharpen their skills, increase their effectiveness, and gain a competitive edge. Presented in a concise, accessible format to save managers valuable time, these books offer authoritative insights and techniques for improving job performance and achieving immediate results.

Other books in the series:

Teams That Click

Presentations That Persuade and Motivate

Face-to-Face Communications for Clarity and Impact

Winning Negotiations That Preserve Relationships

Managing Yourself for the Career You Want

Getting People on Board

Taking Control of Your Time

Dealing with Difficult People

Managing Change to Reduce Resistance

Becoming an Effective Leader

Motivating People for Improved Performance

Hiring Smart for Competitive Advantage

Retaining Your Best People

A Timesaving Guide

THE RESULTS-DRIVEN MANAGER

Creating Breakthrough Innovations

• • •

Harvard Business School Press

Boston, Massachusetts

Copyright 2006 Harvard Business School Publishing Corporation
All rights reserved
Printed in the United States of America
10 09 07 06 05   5 4 3 2 1

Library of Congress Cataloging-in-Publication Data

Creating breakthrough innovations.
        p. cm. — (The results-driven manager series)
     ISBN 1-4221-0183-5
     1. Technological innovations—Management. 2. Creative ability in
business. 3. New products. I. Series.
     HD45.C687 2006
     658.5'14—dc22

                                                      2006003969

The paper used in this publication meets the requirements of the
American National Standard for Permanence of Paper for Publications
and Documents in Libraries and Archives Z39.48-1992.

Contents

Introduction   1

Myths About Innovation

The Road to Disruption 21
Scott D. Anthony and Clayton M. Christensen

Toppling the Walls Surrounding Corporate
Creativity 32
Gary Hamel and Alejandro Sayago

Lost in Translation 45
Anthony W. Ulwick

Six Surprising Insights About Innovation 54
Loren Gary

Applying Innovation Strategies

The New Rules of R&D 65
Henry Chesbrough

Contents

Performance, Convenience, Price: 72
What's Your Brand About?
Scott D. Anthony and Clayton M. Christensen

Where Does the Competitive
Advantage Lie? 86
Loren Gary

Innovation Inside 90
Judith A. Ross

Is Risk the Cost of Innovation? 100
Hal Plotkin

Ambidextrous Innovation 105
Loren Gary

Testing an Idea's Potential

Can You Spot the Sure Winner? 121
Eric Mankin

How to Place Your Best Bets 134
Scott D. Anthony, Mark W. Johnson, and Matt Eyring

Sometimes a Great Notion Isn't Yet a Great
Product 148
Clare Martens

Contents

Is Your Product-Development Process
Helping—or Hindering—Innovation? 156
  Eric Mankin

Disruption Is a Moving Target 168
  Scott D. Anthony

Are You Reading the Right Signals? 179
  Clayton M. Christensen and Scott D. Anthony

About the Contributors   195

Introduction

• • •

No matter what your role is in your organization, you and your employees can contribute to your company's innovativeness—its ability to create new products and services, devise more efficient processes, and design fresh, profitable business models. Innovation is vital to your organization's ongoing health and growth. And when companies grow through innovation, industries and even entire economies grow—raising the standard of living for society.

But despite innovation's value, many managers struggle with the unique challenges presented by this business discipline. For one thing, it's easy to fall victim to all-too-common myths about innovation—such as the belief that innovativeness cannot be taught, that it's only about new technologies or products, that only high-profile industries can be innovative, or that a new idea for a product or process is worthwhile only if it leads to a major breakthrough that alters an entire industry. When managers embrace these myths, they approach innovation in ineffective ways—and their companies pay the price. For example, a manager may push too hard for "big bangs" and miss attractive opportunities that initially seem too trivial to deserve his attention. Or she may pour all her innovation resources into supposed "creative geniuses," depriving her group of the valuable new ideas that other employees could bring to the table if only they were given the chance and the support.

Another challenge takes the form of uncertainty about how, precisely, the innovation process should work. For example, what strategy should you use to generate promising new ideas? Should you search for fresh thinking only within your organization? Or might an analysis of competitors, customers, and other industries also yield valuable insights that could ultimately lead to breakthrough innovations in your own department?

And how should you handle the risks inherent in exploring and experimenting with new ideas? For example, many of the innovative possibilities you and your group generate won't succeed in the market. Even those that do prove commercially successful carry risks. In particular, you may have forged the way with a groundbreaking innovation—only to see rival companies, who were unwilling to shoulder the risks of pioneering an idea, immediately copy your innovation and reap all the benefits. Given these risks, how can you help create a culture that enables you and your employees to feel safe generating and exploring innovative ideas?

But even selecting an effective innovation strategy and putting the right processes and culture in place to support innovation aren't enough. Once you've generated some promising ideas by applying a particular innovation strategy, you still need to test the potential value of those ideas. Only through testing can you figure out which ideas deserve the lion's share of your limited resources.

Yet there's a catch: Testing an idea's potential has grown more complicated than ever. Managers have come under increasing pressure to generate innovations more quickly, yet at the same time, budgets for testing novel ideas are shrinking. If this describes the situation at your company, you need to invest your limited innovation resources shrewdly.

Consider a scenario in which you or several of your employees have envisioned an exciting new product. How do you gauge the possible commercial value of the offering? If you developed the product, what benefits would it offer consumers? Could you price it at a level that would generate a profit for your company? Would the item enable your company to attract entirely new customer segments or exploit a competing company's weaknesses? How likely is it that a competing organization would respond by attacking your new offering with a cheaper, more convenient, or more appealing product? Moreover, as you bring the new idea closer to market, how might you continue to gauge its potential so you'll know immediately whether the product won't succeed after all—and you can "pull the plug" on it before investing too much more?

All of these challenges—understanding and combating myths about innovation, deciding which innovation strategy to use, and testing a new idea's potential—aren't easy to surmount. Yet innovation is so crucial to the health of your company that you need to confront these challenges head-on to generate the results your organization needs to compete and thrive. Written by top-notch experts in the field of innovation—Gary Hamel, Clayton Christensen, Scott Anthony, and Eric Mankin are just a few—the selections in this volume are designed to help you do just that. The articles are organized into three major sections and provide valuable insights and suggestions for removing obstacles to innovation in your group, department, or division. Below is a preview of the concepts, practices, and tools that you'll find as you read this book.

Myths About Innovation

The best way to avoid falling victim to myths about innovation is to understand them. The articles in this section lay out the more common myths, describe their associated costs, and offer more effective mindsets and practices with which to replace widespread myths.

The first selection, "The Road to Disruption" by Scott D. Anthony and Clayton M. Christensen, debunks five innovation myths: 1) *Innovation is all about technology.* The truth is that new ways of doing business, making money, or understanding what customers want are often more valuable forms of innovation than technology. 2) *More resources equal more innovation.* Instead, directing too much money toward innovation can cause teams to fritter away the resources instead of reformulating doomed efforts. 3) *Only a big bang counts as a success.* Rather, most industry-altering innovations start out as small whispers that need time and momentum to become big bangs. 4) *Innovation is random and unpredictable.* Actually, by understanding patterns of success, companies can get innovation right over and over again. 5) *You can't teach innovativeness.* In truth, anyone can learn ways to identify patterns of successful innovation.

In "Toppling the Walls Surrounding Corporate Creativity," Woodside Institute professor Gary Hamel debunks additional innovation-related myths. For example, he challenges the widespread notion that innovation must be locked away in a company's research and development department or new product groups. Instead, every employee must be mobilized to exercise his or her imagination to generate valuable ideas for the company. Hamel also maintains that, contrary to accepted wisdom, innovation doesn't have to be expensive. On the contrary, managers can find low-cost ways of experimenting with new ideas. And indeed, there's "very little correlation between competitive success and R&D expenditure," he writes. And though Hamel agrees that some innovation is risky, just as often, innovation is prudent. He cites the Starbucks debit card as one example: Debit-card technology is well-proven, and the concept could be tested in a few stores before a national rollout. Thus introducing the card was hardly high risk.

In "Lost in Translation," consultant Anthony Ulwick focuses on a particularly destructive myth: the assumption that focus groups and customer surveys will yield accurate information about what types of innovations consumers will value. These practices, Ulwick contends, often generate imprecise conclusions that can lead marketing and development teams astray. Ulwick recommends three tactics for getting—and using—more precise information from consumers: 1) *Find out what jobs potential customers of a particular innovation are trying to accomplish.* For example, some beverages not only quench thirst but also provide vitamins and herbs. 2) *Ask consumers what outcomes they're trying to achieve.* Innovations in oral care products, for instance, have helped people minimize gum irritation. 3) *Identify what's standing in the way of their accomplishing a particular job.* To illustrate, innovative glucose-monitoring test strips enabled diabetics to test their blood more easily, by providing a curved target area for depositing the sample on the strip.

The last article in this section—"Six Surprising Insights About Innovation" by business writer Loren

Gary—challenges additional misguided assumptions, such as the belief that only high-profile industries have a monopoly on innovativeness and that innovation applies only to products. Gary cites the example of Inland Paperboard and Packaging, which demonstrated a truly innovative spirit by overhauling its business model—and scoring a major success. The company found that by "thinking smaller"—creating market-driven regional districts that operated like the independent players in its industry—it could boost profits and serve different customer groups. To make the new business model succeed, the organization had to restructure its sales force and its compensation and production systems. Though risky and radical, the effort paid big dividends. Eventually, it enabled Inland to complete a $900 million acquisition—a move that made it one of the leaders in its industry.

Applying Innovation Strategies

Deciding where and how to generate fresh ideas is a key step in innovating. The articles in this section present a variety of strategies for catalyzing and leveraging new ideas.

In "The New Rules of R&D," Hass School of Business professor Henry Chesbrough advocates looking outside your company, to other firms, so as to leverage ideas that may lead to innovations in your own organization. Some automakers, for example, have begun partnering with suppliers and research outfits to stay on top of new transmission and fuel-cell technologies as well as advances in computer simulation. Knowledge of these technologies enables auto manufacturers to reduce the time required to produce new designs and to experiment with more combinations of the myriad parts that go into a car. Other companies are investing in start-up enterprises that address inefficiencies in their own development processes. Though generating ideas from within is important, looking outward for additional ideas can also be valuable.

Looking outside your company to stimulate innovative ideas can also involve assessing competitors' behavior, as consultant Scott Anthony and Harvard Business School professor Clayton Christensen explain in "Performance, Convenience, Price: What's Your Brand About?" The authors recommend determining whether competing firms are "overshooting"—providing more performance in their products than their customers can utilize. How to tell whether a competitor is overshooting? Its customers are losing their willingness to pay premiums for improvements they once valued, and extra features aren't getting used. Consumers may also have begun complaining that a product is too complicated or costly. If a rival firm is overshooting, you can take advantage of the situation through several means. These include improving the functionality and reliability of your own products, building convenience into your offerings, or providing a "good enough" product at lower prices than the competing company charges.

Loren Gary's article "Where Does the Competitive Advantage Lie?" cites Clayton Christensen's additional ideas for looking outside your company for innovation sources. Consider Big Idea Group, a company that produces only children's toys. The firm conducts "Big Idea Hunts" at regular intervals across the country, inviting inventors from all walks of life to present their ideas to a panel of industry experts. Big Idea's CEO gives constructive feedback on every idea as it's presented.

At relatively low cost, the Hunts have earned a loyal following, have resulted in a growing list of impressive industry contacts, and have enabled the company to generate hundreds of interesting concepts a month. By contrast, many large toy manufacturers discard products sent to them by outside inventors without even looking at them. Because of their hurdle rate—the minimum return required on a contemplated investment—they lack the time and resources to devote to smaller ideas that won't have much chance of wide distribution.

Many companies look both outside and inside to spur innovation. But to unleash the power of ideas within your own organization, you need to develop the right culture and internal processes, as business writer Judith Ross explains in "Innovation Inside." One way is to "cascade a shared commitment to innovation throughout the organization." Whirlpool did this by crafting a new vision, "Innovation from everyone and everywhere," which was led visibly by the CEO. Another tactic entails building rapidly on your company's existing products or concepts; for instance, by reviewing and updating your product line on a seasonal basis and building time into your design cycles for designers to pursue new concepts of their own inspiration. Savvy companies also foster a companywide willingness to learn from both successes and failures while experimenting with new ideas—for example, by tolerating well-intentioned mistakes and rewarding failures that lead to valuable learning.

Business writer Hal Plotkin offers additional advice about building a risk-tolerant culture in "Is Risk the Cost of Innovation?" According to Plotkin, "You need your employees to think innovatively, but you don't want to encourage dumb mistakes or bad business decisions." The best way to draw the line? "Combine a clearly stated policy that anticipates mistakes with a program that conspicuously rewards workers who succeed." For example, Men's Wearhouse augments its mistake-tolerating management approach with a companywide incentive program that motivates employees to experiment with ideas that have never been tried before. Some companies also instruct employees to break down a big, financially risky idea into phases that can be implemented in building-block fashion to test the validity of the employees' assumptions. The key? Make it clear that you expect employees to treat your company's money as their own, and let them know that calculated risks and mistakes won't be fatal to their careers.

The final article in this section—"Ambidextrous Innovation" by Loren Gary—examines a particularly effective strategy for generating innovative ideas within your company. The strategy involves combining incremental improvements in your products and services with bigger changes. To apply this strategy, you need to manage three different "innovation streams": 1) *Incremental innovations*—changes that make your company more competitive in the short term by improving its efficiency. 2) *Architectural innovations*—reconfigurations of existing technology to create process improvements. 3) *Discontinuous innovations*—new operating principles or revolutionary process changes that ensure your company's long-term success.

Ciba Vision, for example, invested in incremental improvements to its current products and processes. It then used the profits from those improvements to fund several autonomous teams. One team was developing entirely new offerings—such as contact lenses that could be worn all day and night. Another was working on a new continuous-production process to radically reduce the cost of manufacturing disposable lenses.

Testing an Idea's Potential

Once you've generated some promising-sounding ideas, you need to determine which of them are most likely to score successes in the marketplace (if they're products or services) or to generate the efficiencies your company is looking for (if they're process innovations). The articles in this section provide helpful guidelines.

In "Can You Spot the Sure Winner?" consultant Eric Mankin describes simple benchmarks that can help you predict the success of a new product or service you're considering developing. To succeed, a new offering must meet four criteria: 1) It's less expensive than existing products. 2) It offers greater benefits. 3) It's easy for consumers to use. 4) It's readily available and easy to buy. Procter & Gamble used these benchmarks to identify the high potential of its electric toothbrush, the SpinBrush. The product sold for $5, versus competitors' $50. Because it ran on disposable batteries, it offered portability as a benefit. Its straightforward design made it easy to use. And P&G's strong distribution capabilities made it easy to buy. Like the SpinBrush, a product that excels along all four criteria stands a strong chance of being a winner.

In "How to Place Your Best Bets," consultants Scott Anthony, Mark Johnson, and Matt Eyring present another model for gauging a new idea's potential. Likely winners, the authors contend, will appeal to "over-served" customers (those who consume an offering but don't need all its features or customers) by providing satisfactory performance at lower prices and more convenience. High-potential offerings can also attract "non-consumers"—people who lack the wealth needed to participate in a market or who can use a product or service only in an inconvenient setting.

Another criterion for a winning idea is that it will appeal in markets that competing companies are ignoring or want to exit in order to find higher-margin opportunities up-market. How to identify these competitors? Examine rival firms' income statements, balance sheets, history of investment decisions, and customer behaviors. Based on this information, identify new offerings your company could develop that won't likely trigger a response from competitors.

If your company is under pressure to generate new offerings more quickly but has limited budgets for testing new ideas, you'll want to read business journalist Clare Martens' article "Sometimes a Great Notion Isn't Yet a Great Product." The article provides eight tips for deriving maximum value from your idea testing. For example, avoid testing too early or too late in an idea's development cycle. Otherwise, you may end up with wildly misleading results. Test only at those development points where consumers can have meaningful experiences with the idea—for instance, by inviting consumers' feedback on a product sketch or prototype. Another tip is to seek naive users to serve as your testers. People who are totally unfamiliar with a potential product or service are better at figuring out how to use the device or service. Thus they can give you more meaningful feedback about how the offering functions.

Idea testing is most effective when it's iterative, as Eric Mankin points out in "Is Your Product-Development Process Helping—or Hindering—Innovation?" By conducting many tests and experiments during an idea's development, you repeatedly garner feedback about the potential offering that you can use to refine the idea so that it stands the best chance of succeeding.

To illustrate, a consumer-electronics firm called Danger used this process to develop its hugely successful hiptop2 device, a super cell phone. The hiptop2 began as a tiny, cheap personal digital assistant that could fit on a key chain and that was connected to a computer via a small dock. The company took this version to investors, who asked the designers to make it wireless. Once the product was wireless, investors suggested giving it two-way communication. The final incarnation of the product was a $300 all-in-one communication device that boasts a color screen and camera and that serves as a phone, Internet browser, e-mail device, personal organizer, and instant-messaging apparatus.

In "Disruption Is a Moving Target," Scott Anthony focuses on the notion that a new idea has greater potential if it's not likely to trigger attacks (in the form of competing products or lower prices) from rival companies. The key to making this determination is to identify a potential innovation to which rivals either don't want to—or can't—respond.

For example, innovations that attract a rival company's least profitable customers stand a better chance of not triggering an attack. By offering such a product or service, you put rival companies in a position of having to decide whether to invest to defend their least profitable business, or invest to produce better offerings that allow them to charge higher prices to more demanding customers at their market's high end. The natural inclination is to let the lower-end business go.

The final article in this section—"Are You Reading the Right Signals?" by Clayton Christensen and Scott Anthony—provides a case study of how to test a new idea's potential. The authors describe three new ideas emerging in the telecommunications industry: 1) free Internet-based telephony services, 2) high-speed "fixed wireless" broadband solutions, and 3) use of instant messaging to hold audio conferences and videoconferences. They then evaluate these ideas' potential.

For instance, if Skype, the newly formed company considering developing free Internet-based telephony services, plans to make money by selling services (such as voicemail) and advertisements, incumbents would have to give away their core product in order to compete. Thus rivals won't likely respond to development of this idea. On the other hand, Skype has attracted investment from top-shelf venture capitalists—who may insist on rapid growth. This pressure might force Skype to target large, existing markets instead of trying to create new markets—which could limit the idea's potential.

* * *

Clearly, you need to keep many considerations in mind while using innovation to fuel valuable results for your company. As you read the articles in this book, carefully weigh the following questions:

- Which myths about innovation do you tend to hold? How does believing in those myths affect the way you manage innovation in your group or department? Which of the alternative mindsets and practices described in the section "Myths About Innovation" would best enable you to improve your management of innovation?

- Where do you look for promising new ideas? Do you look inside your company only? To competing firms' behavior? To independent entrepreneurs and inventors seeking a home for their ideas? How might you broaden your search to ensure the best results?

- What do you do to ensure that your employees feel safe exploring and experimenting with new ideas? What new processes, systems, and cultural changes might you initiate to encourage employees to take risks while also avoiding overly costly mistakes?

- How are new ideas' potential tested in your group, department, or company? What criteria are used to identify the most likely winners in a list of ideas? From whom do you and other managers gather feedback during the development of a promising idea? And when do you gather feedback? What changes in your idea-testing approaches might help you increase the odds of picking winners?

Myths About Innovation

. . .

The best way to avoid falling victim to myths about innovation is to understand them. The articles that follow lay out the more common myths, describe their associated costs, and offer more effective mindsets.

In these pages, you'll discover an abundance of surprising realities about innovation. For example, it's not all about technology. It doesn't have to be expensive. And it can be taught. Moreover, a breakthrough innovation often starts out as a small whisper, not a big bang. Innovation can occur in every industry, not just the high-profile ones. And it's not only about products: Organizational processes, services, and business models can be innovative as well.

The Road to Disruption

• • •

Scott D. Anthony and Clayton M. Christensen

Innovation Myths

Everyone knows that innovation is vital to an organization's ongoing health. Indeed, the creation of new products, services, processes, and profit models fuels the growth not just of companies but of national and global economies.

It is amazing that such an important discipline is so misunderstood. Statements such as "Innovation is a random event," "Innovation is intrinsic and can't be taught," and "If we could just spend more money, we could be more innovative" are often heard echoing down corporate hallways.

Not only are these and other such statements false, but they also stand in the way of companies' ability to grapple with some of the legitimate—but surmountable—challenges related to innovation. Since the first step to recovery is acknowledgement, we begin by highlighting and debunking some of the most common myths that impede companies' quest to master innovation.

Myth 1: Innovation is all about technology.

What makes Dell and Wal-Mart great companies? Sure, they use technology, but their core competitive advantage resides in their business models, the way they organize to create and capture value. Why has Procter & Gamble had so much success lately? The company employs great technologists, for sure, but its deep understanding of consumer needs and its ability to implement the findings it garners from that understanding helps Procter & Gamble point those technologists in the right direction.

There's no question that technology is important, but many times it is the icing on the cake. Innovation is also about new ways of doing business, new ways of making money, and new ways of understanding what customers want.

Myth 2: More resources equal more innovation.

Managers often think that allocating more resources toward developing and introducing products will solve all their innovation problems. However, directing too much money toward innovation can actually stand in the way of success. Teams often fritter away extra money, wandering aimlessly down fruitless paths instead of shutting down or reformulating doomed efforts. The problems often reside in the way in which the resources are allocated and managed, not the resources themselves.

Myth 3: Only a big bang counts as a success.

Most industry-altering innovations actually start out as small whispers. It takes time and plenty of momentum before they become big bangs. Companies that push too hard for big bangs—to the exclusion of initially smaller prospects—can miss extremely attractive opportunities that at first appear to be too trivial to matter.

Myth 4: Innovation—and the growth that results from it—is simply random and unpredictable.

Undeniably, serendipitous occurrences can be key components of success, but innovation is significantly more predictable than most people believe. There are patterns of success that, if properly understood and followed, can greatly increase a company's chances of getting it right over and over again. Just because those patterns are hard to see or not well understood does not mean they do not exist. Remember, 30 years ago, many people believed that achieving total quality within the manufacturing process was inherently random. The quality movement showed that was not the case.

Myth 5: You can't teach people how to be more innovative.

This myth builds off another misconception, that innovation requires a creative genius to spearhead it, someone who just has the right stuff. In truth, because innovations follow distinct patterns, anyone (and everyone) can learn specific ways to identify those patterns and proceed appropriately. It is a challenge, no doubt, but one very much worth undertaking.

Key Principles of Disruptive Innovation

Debunking the myths of innovation requires identifying the patterns that separate high-potential innovation strategies from low-potential approaches. *The Innovator's Solution: Creating and Sustaining Successful Growth,* by Clayton M. Christensen and Michael E. Raynor, suggests that the highest-potential route to building a new-growth business is creating a disruptive innovation that brings simple, cheap, convenient solutions to overshot customers at the low end of an established market or, alternatively, brings the same types of solutions to nonconsumers who lack the skills, wealth, or ability to get an important job done themselves.

Disruptive innovations have affected and will continue to affect a number of different marketplaces. Consider the automotive industry. Toyota created disruptive growth by entering the low end of the market with the inexpensive Corona model in the 1960s. Over the succeeding three decades, the company has progressively moved up-market to the point where it now has a reputation for producing some of the highest-performing cars in the world. Korean auto manufacturers such as Hyundai and Kia have lately stepped into the void, competing at the low end of existing markets.

Looming on the horizon are emerging minivehicle makers in developing economies. For example, India's Tata Motors, the automotive arm of the Mumbai, India–based Tata Group conglomerate best known for its business process outsourcing offering, plans to introduce a $2,200 compact car in 2008. Tata hopes it can tap into the vast pool of Indian nonconsumers. If the strategy succeeds, it will build a platform that could ease Tata's disruptive expansion into other higher-end markets.

Disruptive developments are in the process of transforming several industries. For example:

- In health care, companies are introducing quick and convenient diagnostic and prescription services delivered by nurse practitioners in kiosks located in retail stores. The leading example of this emerging model is Minnesota-based MinuteClinic, whose nurse practitioner–staffed kiosks offer efficient and effective treatment for more than a dozen of the most common ailments, such as strep throat and ear infections.

- In telecommunications, a technology known as voice over Internet protocol (VoIP) now allows companies to offer cheap, customizable telephony service over the Internet. Vonage is the leading standalone provider, but market incumbents such as Verizon are also trying to introduce similar models.

- In aviation, several players are racing to create very low-cost airplanes that will enable the birth of a vibrant air-taxi industry. Start-ups such as Eclipse Aviation and Adam Aircraft, corporate jet manufacturers such as Cessna, and automobile manufacturers such as Honda are all targeting the space.

- In education, on-the-job training and online adult education providers are delivering extremely relevant, low-cost academic opportunities in more convenient settings. Obvious examples of this trend include General Electric's Crotonville, N.Y., training center and the University of Phoenix, which offers classes to working adults in the classroom and over the Internet.

- In the software arena, countless companies are designing flexible, nonproprietary, and low-cost software offerings based on the Linux operating system. For example, MySQL has developed the popular open-source database software offering that has more than 10 million active installations.

- In consumer electronics, cellular phones and home gaming systems are continuing their assault on other devices. Cameras on cellular phones have gotten so sophisticated so quickly that they are already affecting the sales of standalone digital cameras. Home gaming systems such as Sony's PlayStation 2 and Microsoft's Xbox are adding additional features that move computing from the office to the family room.

Disruptive approaches such as the ones detailed above have two core benefits. They strike a chord with an overlooked or overshot customer, and they do so in a way that doesn't fit the processes and profit models of market incumbents. Because disruptive concepts face far less competition from incumbents than concepts viewed as "sustaining," they have a higher probability of marketplace success.

New Mindsets Required to Unleash Disruptive Innovations

Despite the best of intentions within many companies, existing beliefs—embodied by the innovation myths mentioned above—are a major barrier to creating disruptive growth. There are four new mindsets that companies need to adopt to increase their odds of catching disruptive growth.

Mindset 1: The right metrics at the right time.

Project teams need to focus on metrics that recognize the inherent uncertainty in the early days of a new venture. Teams often focus too much on meaningless metrics such as net-present-value or return-on-investment figures during a project's early stages. These numbers can be critical tools for evaluating projects—but only after there is more certainty about the approach and the market.

When a team is still operating largely based on assumptions, intuition, and guesswork, it should be evaluating how closely an opportunity fits a defined pattern rather than relying on numbers in which it can have little confidence.

Mindset 2: Uncertainty should be embraced.

Almost all true new-growth initiatives will have high degrees of uncertainty. Project teams often implicitly penalize any ambiguous opportunity. As a result, they feel an almost gravitational pull toward low-risk, low-return options. Managers should encourage teams to embrace uncertainty while simultaneously running the experiments that will stamp it out.

People tend to think of successful entrepreneurs as risk-tolerant individuals. In reality, many of the best entrepreneurs seek to minimize risk as much as possible, finding partners and creative ways to systematically remove the risk factors from an opportunity.

Mindset 3: Failure can be a good thing.

Fear of failure makes it very difficult for companies to venture down uncharted paths. Most managers think, "If I fail, I will be branded with a scarlet 'F,' which will limit my ability to continue to advance through the organization."

Not all failures are created equal, though. If a manager

does something obviously foolish and fails, and then repeats that mistake again and again, companies should certainly react appropriately. But organizations should encourage the right type of failure, one that results in a vital piece of learning. For example, a team that quickly discovers its strategy is not viable and recommends canning the project has done its company a great service. The team has helped to ensure that the company's scarce resources are allocated more appropriately.

Mindset 4: Scarcity can be an advantage.

Many companies attempt to drown their most promising opportunities with generous capital allocations. Yet, as discussed earlier, giving a team too many resources can actually be a root cause of failure.

Managers should remember that scarcity is the entrepreneur's advantage. Entrepreneurs are forced to think of creative ways around obstacles because they have no other option. The curse of too much capital leads many teams to spend too much time and energy running in a fatally flawed direction. In general, the best new-growth opportunities should be starved of resources. Companies should give project teams enough money to test initial assumptions but nothing more.

Summary: New mindsets need new processes.

Creating these new mindsets is never easy. At most companies, misbegotten mindsets influence the processes used to allocate and manage resources, thwarting managers with even the very best of intentions. This is why we often suggest that companies create separate processes dedicated to shaping and nurturing disruptive innovations.

With more of a blank slate, companies can put in place processes that embody the right principles and mindsets. As the new processes demonstrate success, they can catalyze wider organizational change.

Toppling the Walls Surrounding Corporate Creativity

• • •

Gary Hamel and Alejandro Sayago

At a recent Harvard Business School Publishing conference, Gary Hamel—visiting professor of strategic and international management at the London Business School and chairman of the Woodside Institute, a foundation whose mission is to advance organizational resilience, innovation, and renewal—spoke about the myths that get in the way of innovation within business organizations. At the same conference, Alejandro Sayago, innovation processes director for CEMEX, Mexico's cement giant, described his own organization's highly successful efforts to ensure that innovation is an integral part of the company's DNA and at the forefront of every employee's consciousness. Below are excerpts from each of their presentations.

Gary Hamel's Eight Innovation Myths

Myth 1: Big ideas start out big.

No truly big idea ever starts as a big idea. It takes a lot of crazy, wacky, small ideas to find a few initiatives worth experimenting with, which may then allow you to find a few things that are truly worth investing in and could ultimately lead to one or two winners.

One of the challenges for a lot of organizations is that they don't have this approach to strategy. They don't think about strategy as a numbers game in which the likelihood of generating a rule-breaking idea is totally dependent on the number of way-out ideas the company created at the start. In fact, most companies would like to believe that they can avoid the experiments and the semi-failed projects by putting some really smart people in a room for a few days and asking them to think really hard.

This is just one myth that gets in the way of a company's innovation potential. There are, in my estimation, seven other myths that trip up corporate creativity.

Myth 2: Innovation is mostly about products.

That's way too limiting. There's the capability for innovation along every single aspect of the business model. It's about pricing. It's about how vertically integrated you are. It's about how you manage the customer relationship. And that's just for starters.

Myth 3: Innovation is about the top line.

It's typically focused on creating new products and services that will drive top-line growth. But radical innovation in the cost structure is equally vital. Dell, JetBlue, and eTrade are just a few of the companies that have succeeded in dramatically rethinking traditional cost structures. Incremental cost cutting is no substitute for innovation that takes big chunks out of an industry's traditional cost structure.

Myth 4: Innovation can't be taught.

Actually, it can. It is entirely possible to teach people how to challenge innovation-stifling industry conventions, how to uncover the unspoken frustrations and needs of customers that can illuminate new innovation opportunities, and how to understand opportunities to leverage environmental trends and discontinuities that have gone unexploited by competitors. Whirlpool, for one, has trained thousands of employees to be business innovators. Indeed, every salaried employee is required to complete a basic instructional module on the basics of innovative thinking. Mexico's CEMEX has a variety of processes in place to foster innovation.

Myth 5: Innovation isn't my job.

In a world where the returns on incremental improvements are diminishing relative to the returns on full-scale innovation, breakthrough thinking is everyone's responsibility. Innovation can't be locked up in R&D and new product development but must be a widely distributed capability. The goal is simple: to mobilize and monetize the imagination of every single employee.

Myth 6: Innovation is risky.

This is another typical misconception—and as long as it holds sway, innovation will be a second-class citizen. Sure, some innovation is risky—like GM's bet on hydrogen-powered cars, for instance. But just as often, innovation is prudent. Consider the Starbucks debit card. This was real innovation: no one in the fast-food industry had ever before convinced customers to prepay for their morning latte and muffin. Yet the innovation was hardly high risk. Debit-card technology is well proven, and the concept could be tested in a few stores before a national rollout. Risk is a function of investment multiplied by uncertainty. The trick, of course, is to innovate in ways that don't require bet-the-farm investments.

Myth 7: Innovation is expensive.

Not necessarily. You have to find low-cost ways of experimenting. Figure out how to get a lot more innovation for a whole lot less investment. We know there is very little correlation between competitive success and R&D expenditure—whether you measure it by pure R&D dollars, whether you measure it by R&D as a percentage of sales, or whether you measure it by path to success.

Rather, the question is, What proportion of the total imagination in my company am I exploiting? How many of your employees would wake up tomorrow saying, "I understand that I have a responsibility for business innovation"?

Myth 8: Innovation is an exception.

Like the push for quality 40 years ago, innovation is not the norm in many organizations. But, like quality, it can become a systemic capability rather than the preserve of a particular function. Building a capability requires attention to training, tools, metrics, decision processes, incentives, and organizational values. Only when all these things support continuous rule-breaking innovation will innovation become a way of life rather than an occasional and exceptional activity.

How CEMEX Innovates

Innovation by Committee

About four years ago, CEMEX realized it needed to develop new formulas for growth in markets where our presence was already strong. In some of our key markets—such as Mexico—we already owned a significant market share but knew those numbers weren't going to go much higher. We also knew that our competitors were making greater inroads, increasing their output of cement, and becoming more aggressive about challenging our leadership position.

If we were still going to deliver growth, we had to be proactive. So we embarked on a journey of innovation. We developed a model for internal processes that would enable us to foster innovation across the company. The model embeds innovation in the organization so new projects would not necessarily be a consequence of serendipity but, rather, the result of an ongoing, deliberate pipeline.

A key element of our model is the *innovation committee*. Through this committee we establish our strategy—what we want to innovate toward.

Since we are in the cement and ready-mix business, essentially we're in the construction business, and we don't want to develop too far from that core. So, it's important that we set up an agenda for where we want to focus our efforts. That happens through the innovation committee, which comprises nine top people: four vice presidents, four directors, and one external consultant who knows the company well. These individuals, representing most of the divisions of CEMEX Mexico, participate on a rotating basis, with changes occurring every 12 to 18 months.

Of course, strategy isn't enough. We have to walk the talk. So, we devised processes to deliver new business initiatives. We have two processes. The first we call *innovation platforms,* the second we call the *idea bank.*

Innovation Platforms

Innovation platforms are essentially themes that we use to innovate upon. For example, one of these themes is "Integrated Construction Solutions." Under this heading, anything that can make construction faster, leaner, or more productive is of interest. We look for business opportunities that could be developed around that particular idea. Another recent theme was "Regional Economic Development." What can we do to foster regional and economic development that could also become a source of business for us? We operate multiple platforms simultaneously, with specific focus on construction solutions; product delivery, logistics, and associated services; and new application development for cement and concrete.

Each platform is developed using the following stages:

Opportunity search. First we look for opportunities under our theme. So, if we're talking about regional development, we ask, "What kinds of opportunities are out there in regional and economic development that we can take advantage of?"

Exploration. We explore a variety of things based on what is going on in the local, national, or global economy. We'll look at things like trends in demographics, what new technologies are available that we could somehow harness, and so forth. The point is to zero in on two or three good, solid opportunities that are interesting to pursue—the types of opportunities that could change the industry or could change the dynamics of what we're doing and give us a competitive advantage if we were able to solve that opportunity.

Ideation. Then we move into what we call the ideation stage. This is where most of the creative work takes place. So now we have this opportunity. How do we take advantage of it? What types of things can we do with it? There is no secret formula behind ideation, but there are a number of tools we use to help flesh out an idea. For example, one approach we have used in the past is a "Ping-Pong" tournament.

This means we place the opportunity in front of a group of about 32 employees from all over the company at every level, and we draw a starting pairing. For example, Eric will play a round of "Ping-Pong" with Vic during the week. They will try to come up with ideas to take advantage of the opportunity we've identified. Eric will "serve" by sending his first idea to Vic. Vic will have 24 hours to respond to that idea by either fleshing it out or by building on it. Vic and Eric continue to bounce ideas back and forth for two or three rounds, usually within a week's time frame. And everything is being captured on an Internet-based system.

At the end of a week, a panel of experts will judge Eric's and Vic's ideas and will determine who won that particular game. If Vic was the winner, he'll go on to play another round with the next person in the group. (The competition takes place with pseudonyms so there are no hard feelings over who won and who lost.) By the end of the game—which can last for five weeks or so—not only are you going to have a very motivated group of people thinking about a business opportunity, but you are also going to have a whole bunch of new ideas. And when people get competitive about this game—which they do—they really come up with some pretty interesting suggestions.

Filtering. Once we have a portfolio of five or six solid ideas, we move into the next phase of the process, filtering the ideas and determining which ones could actually become viable business concepts. At this stage we usually involve insightful colleagues who possess the knowledge, experience, and imagination to transform ideas into true business concepts. These individuals come from within or outside the organization and are usually experts in the industry. This stage is where we identify what the product and the solution are, answering such questions as: What is the target market? What's going on within that target market? Is it growing? Is it expanding? What are the benefits that we can offer through the product or service, whether they be functional, economic, or psychological? We try to identify what key success factors would enable that idea to pan out.

Development. Once we've translated an idea into a business concept, we take the concept back to the innovation committee and decide if the concept has enough punch to drive it through the next step. This could mean launching a pilot, developing a business plan, or sponsoring a more serious study into its viability. Finally, whenever we identify something that looks to have the potential to be very successful, we will roll it out.

Some pretty interesting things have come out of this process. A good example is what we call *accelerated construction.* In Mexico, and in many developing countries, housing is a big issue, and providing housing for lower- and middle-income families is critical. Right now, there is a huge government program to try to foster such housing. In fact, a lot of private and government funds are flowing to that particular segment. So we began thinking about how we could use the opportunity and turn it into a business. We've talked with customers. We did a lot of things to identify what opportunities existed within that segment.

One customer articulated something quite insightful to us. He said, "My biggest concern is human labor. Due to the scarcity of skilled labor in a given region, we have had to fly experienced people from different parts of the country to help us build a housing project." Through our internal innovation process we thought about it and someone said, "Why don't we use metallic molds, the type that are used to make big warehouses?" We just pour concrete into those molds. Those things can be assembled in just a few hours. We could do that for a small home, for the type of homes required for this initiative.

After the concrete sets, we remove the molds and you have an almost-completed house. We did some piloting of the idea and launched the business a little over 24 months ago. Last year the idea produced close to $30 million of economic benefits for the company through year-end. It gives the customer a great solution because the builder was able to reduce the construction cycle from 24 days to three days. Plus, the homeowner gets a quality house. Errors such as crooked walls are reduced. And the method uses more cement per square foot of construction than traditional methods. So, it's a three-way win.

Idea Bank

Our second process is somewhat different. We call it the *idea bank*. This is another Internet-based system where anyone in the organization—absolutely anyone—can submit an idea. It has to be a business idea, and when you submit an idea you have to explain what the benefits are, what the costs are, what the implications are, what the key success factors are, and how the company would implement it. So it forces the individual to think about the idea before bringing it up.

We create a portfolio of the ideas we receive that we group by different business units. And within each one of those portfolios, the ideas fall into one of four categories. Each idea is designated as a star, a ball, an apple, or a bone.

If the idea has a lot of potential and could also be relatively easy to implement, it's a *star*. Those ideas you want to go ahead and pursue immediately.

If the idea is something that could have a lot of business potential, but we're not really quite sure how to implement it now, we'll call the idea a *ball* because we still have to bounce it around before we find a way to benefit from it.

If the idea has relatively low value yet it's easy to implement, we'll call it an *apple*. We'll give that apple to whoever is the right individual in the organization, and he or she can decide whether to chew on it or throw it away.

Finally, for ideas that are designated as *bones,* we'll look for any meat on them, and even if we're never able to find any, we'll still keep those ideas.

Last year alone, we were able to obtain 1,800 submissions from all over the organization. Out of those 1,800 submissions, about 210 ideas were deemed valuable. Of course, you're going to get a whole bunch of ideas that really belong to continuous improvement, which is fine.

The platforms are usually staffed with 10 to 12 people who generally give us about 20% of their time—one day per week. They come from all over the organization, which means we are able to obtain input from all over the company. The projects gain ownership much more quickly this way, rather than just having an isolated incubator that's on its own, doing its own thing.

Reprint S0411B

Lost in Translation

. . .

Anthony W. Ulwick

Many companies take great pride in allocating significant portions of their annual budgets toward conducting customer interviews as the primary route to improving products and services. Yet this traditional, customer-driven process is fraught with ambiguity and often leads to failure.

No one intends to mislead. Companies, for their part, generally don't seem to know the right questions to ask, nor do they always know what to do with the information they receive. Customers, though perfectly willing to share their "requirements," are unaware of what information the company really needs.

Ultimately, companies—lacking any knowledge of what inputs are needed—accept the imprecise statements they get from customers and then have marketing and development teams "translate" them to make them more useful. But interpreting these inputs only introduces more variability into the process.

However, the right kind of customer feedback ensures that all participants in the feedback process are speaking the same language. Knowing how to get this feedback and how to apply it will help you successfully grow new and existing markets.

Feedback Fundamentals

We have identified three distinct types of inputs that are fundamental to the innovation process and its successful execution. To create a breakthrough product or service or to successfully enter a new market, a company must know:

1. What jobs the customer is trying to get done.

2. The outcomes the customer is trying to achieve when performing these jobs in a variety of circumstances.

3. The constraints that stand in the way of the adoption of a new product or service.

1. Jobs to be done: A key input for growth.

Customers—consumers and companies alike—buy products and services when they need help getting a job done. When faced with the job of removing food from their teeth, for example, people may purchase a toothbrush and toothpaste or dental floss. Understanding what job a customer wants to get done with a product or service is critical to the product's success. Less obvious, however, are the growth possibilities that may result from knowing what supporting, ancillary, or related jobs customers want done in conjunction with the primary job of interest.

Offering solutions that address additional jobs frequently results in the creation of a breakthrough product or service. For example, beverage producers have started putting out products that not only quench thirst but also enable users to obtain vitamins, nutrients, and herbs that may improve performance in given situations. SoBe Beverages, Red Bull Energy Drink, and Glaceau Vitamin Water address the related functional jobs customers want the drinks to perform when quenching their thirst. Such products now account for a sizable percentage of beverage sales.

Customers often want a product or service to perform more than one job at a time. Yet companies tend to focus their offerings on only one job because addressing the ancillary jobs often necessitates developing new or different competencies or crossing organizational boundaries. While developing these competencies may indeed require new skills and investment, addressing all the jobs customers are trying to get a product or service to do under a given set of circumstances can certainly pay great dividends.

2. Desired outcomes: Metrics that drive innovation.

In addition to wanting to get more jobs done, customers want to get a specific job done more efficiently. By providing them the means to do so, a company creates value. The first step in this process is capturing from customers the metrics, or measures of value, that define how they want to get the job done and what it means to get the job done perfectly. We call these metrics the customer's *desired outcomes*.

When executing the job of removing food from teeth, for example, customers may want to:

- Minimize the time it takes to prepare the teeth for cleaning.

- Minimize the time it takes to remove food from hard-to-reach places.

- Minimize the number of passes that must be made to remove all food particles.

- Minimize the likelihood of gum irritation.

- Minimize the likelihood of wearing down the teeth.

- Minimize the number of teeth that cannot be reached.

- Minimize the frequency with which food removal is required.

It should also be noted that desired outcomes, when captured correctly, are stable over time, differentiating them from other types of requirements. People who were cleaning their teeth back in the 1950s, for example, wanted to minimize the time it took to remove food from hard-to-reach places and decrease the likelihood of gum irritation—just as people do today and will in the future. Desired outcomes have this unique quality because they are fundamental measures of performance inherent to the execution of a specific job. Indeed, they will be valid metrics for as long as customers are trying to get that job done. Consequently, knowing what outcomes customers are trying to achieve gives a company short-term as well as long-term direction in selecting which ideas and technologies to pursue.

The outcomes that should be the focus for improvement, however, do change over time as new and better technologies are introduced. When angled handles and brushes were incorporated into toothbrushes, for example, users were better satisfied with their ability to minimize the time it takes to remove food from hard-to-reach places. This meant that the opportunity to create new value along that dimension was diminished and that manufacturers had to determine which other outcomes were important and unsatisfied before new value could be created.

Getting the Goods

Much controversy exists around how best to garner customer inputs. Some tout the benefits of personal interviews and focus groups, while others favor ethnographic, anthropological, or observational research. In truth, success is not dependent on the method used but in knowing what inputs you want to get from customers when engaging in the requirements-gathering process.

When AIG, the U.S.-based international insurer and financial services organization, used our outcome-driven innovation methods to improve its agent service offering in the division that finances premium payments for businesses paying large premiums, it chose to employ a combination of one-on-one and group interviews. AIG interviewed 30 financing agents who use AIG's and/or a competitor's services, taking four weeks to complete the process.

The interviewer focused the discussion with the agents on the activities associated with the job of setting up and managing a customer account. For example, agents were asked to discuss what they were trying to achieve when obtaining quotes, preparing agreements, gathering approvals, managing overdue accounts, posting payments, and reinstating policies.

To identify the agents' desired outcomes, the interviewer instructed the agents to think through the process of conducting each of the above-named activities during a typical day as they obtained offerings from different insurance companies. For example, agents were asked, "What makes one insurance company's offering better or worse than another and why? What characteristics describe the 'ideal' service offering?" By forcing this type of discussion, the interviewer was able to get the agents to state the criteria they use to evaluate the performance of one offering over another. These criteria were the agents' desired outcomes.

Rather than transcribing all the interviews, then later searching through hundreds of pages for interesting tidbits, the interviewer captured the outcomes during the interview by typing them directly into a PC and validating their accuracy and completeness with the agents in real time.

Each session ended with three to four pages of statements that were classified as outcomes, jobs, or constraints. Any ambiguities were discussed with the agents and clarified during the session to ensure that statements would not have to be interpreted or amended later on. After several sessions, the compiled statements were netted out so duplicate information could be removed. In the end, AIG obtained approximately 75 statements that reflected the way in which its customers measure value when setting up and managing accounts. The resulting inputs were subsequently prioritized and used to guide idea generation and concept evaluation, leading to the creation of a new service offering. The new service was instituted in late 2003 and includes innovative features that are winning AIG new business.

3. Constraints: Roadblocks to success.

Another way to create value is by helping customers overcome constraints that inhibit them from getting a job done. Consider, for example, how Roche became the market leader in glucose-monitoring test strips after lagging for years behind Johnson & Johnson's LifeScan division. LifeScan test strips, like others on the market, required a user to place a blood sample on the top of the test strip. If a diabetic were experiencing shaky hands and blurred vision as a result of a diabetic episode, this could become difficult. Thus, when he needed the product the most, it was more difficult to use.

Roche saw an opportunity in this constraint. In 1998, the company introduced Accu-Chek Comfort Curve test strips, which have a curved target area that allows for easier placement of the blood sample, thus enabling diabetic patients to easily take readings even when suffering from diabetic episodes. This innovative product helped Roche take over market leadership from Johnson & Johnson's LifeScan division by the end of 2003.

It is common for numerous constraints to stand in the way of product use or adoption. Determining why a product or service would not be used—even if it satisfied all the stated outcomes—identifies a third, often very promising avenue for potential growth.

Transforming Innovation

When dealing with the innovation process, managers need a common language with which to discuss issues and build a shared understanding. Currently, few employees in any company know all or even most of the jobs customers are trying to get done, the outcomes they're trying to achieve, or the constraints they're trying to overcome. Improvement in the development process is inevitable when everyone across a given company has access to this valuable information and is empowered and motivated to use it to create customer value.

Reprint S0405A

Six Surprising Insights About Innovation

• • •

Loren Gary

Don't let drabness fool you, whether it's the company's industry, location, or product line. Firms in high-profile industries such as telecommunications or biotech don't have a monopoly on creativity. Sometimes companies operating out of the media spotlight, in sectors that are decidedly not high-tech, can teach you a surprising amount about innovation.

In the 1990s, overcapacity in the paper industry was causing prices to erode. Inland Paperboard and Packaging (Indianapolis), the largest unit of the Austin conglomerate Temple-Inland, was in a bind. With $2 billion in annual revenue, Inland was in the middle of the pack, neither a niche player nor a market leader. With its future hanging in the balance, Inland's leadership decided to challenge the fundamental assumptions of its business model.

"The big integrated companies take it for granted that you drive for scale to compete on cost," says Inland CFO Mike Sullivan. "Their incentive systems encourage the production of as many tons of paper as possible with the mills running at full capacity. But we challenged the thinking that the lowest cost per ton equals more profit; we wanted the marketplace to tell the mills when to run instead of the other way around. To improve our results and become a greater force in the industry, we had to think smaller. We created market-driven regional districts that operated like the independent players in our industry. We changed metrics and compensation away from cost per ton to ROI. These incentives forced the district managers to create new approaches. We also realigned our asset base by closing one mill and putting another into a joint venture making high-value products for a different industry; these changes brought better balance to our supply chain."

Profits ultimately rebounded, and Inland recently completed a $900 million acquisition, making it one of the leaders in the industry. But the strategy was a very risky one, especially in a down cycle, explains Robert J. Thomas, senior fellow at Accenture's Institute for Strategic Change.

"To pull it off, Inland had to turn almost everything in the unit 180 degrees—starting with the sales force and the way it was compensated, and continuing right on through to the production operation. Inland was doing things that were riskier and more creative than much of what goes on in Silicon Valley."

Innovation springs from the unlikeliest of companies—and people.

This lesson from Inland is just one of the counterintuitive insights about innovation discussed at a recent forum sponsored by Harvard Business School Publishing. Here are a few others that grew out of that gathering, augmented by additional sources.

Constraints can sometimes spur rather than impede creativity.

Easy access to capital and the absence of time pressure do not guarantee innovative outcomes. Inland made its game-changing moves when it was under the gun—money was scarce and the need to take action was immediate. Says Randy Komisar, the start-up incubator, virtual CEO, and author of *The Monk and the Riddle:* "In a company that's experiencing a slight slowdown, but where this slowdown hasn't been reflected yet in the stock price and investors are still showing confidence, someone who comes on board as a new CEO has his hands tied—he's almost forced to stay the course. Companies, especially large ones, are often better innovators when their backs are against the wall."

Not feeling enough pressure may have been Maytag's problem when it tried to position itself to take advantage of fast-developing technologies related to household appliances. Maytag wanted to be able to cash in if any of these technologies turned out to be a real breakthrough. Putting its eggs in a bunch of different baskets, Maytag avoided the risk associated with studying the various alternatives more carefully and determining the one best bet to focus on. But this middle-of-the-road, low-risk strategy ensured middling, low-impact results. "It probably hastened CEO Lloyd Ward's departure from office," says Thomas.

Look for happy people—then provoke them into an argument.

"There's a lot of evidence to suggest that optimists are more persistent in the face of adversity," says Robert I. Sutton, professor of management science and engineering at the Stanford Engineering School, where he co-directs the Center for Work, Technology, and Organization. In addition, Sutton writes in *Weird Ideas That Work,* when people are in a good mood, they are more cognitively flexible: "They generate more varied ideas and combinations of those ideas." Once you've got a group of happy, optimistic people working on a business idea, encourage them to question one another's assumptions. When an idea "is beyond its infancy, but still unproven, constructive conflict is crucial for developing and testing its value," Sutton writes. Constructive conflict has very definite hallmarks, he continues; it's when people are arguing over "ideas rather than personality or relationship issues."

Innovation isn't always a companywide phenomenon.

"In many firms in which there's a lot of emphasis on being first to market with a new technology, once that technology sorts itself out, companywide performance tends to recede to less-than-impressive levels," says Thomas. "In many seemingly drab, established companies, however, you'll find pockets of innovation that occur without explicit sanctioning." In other words, instead of insisting that creativity be sky-high at all times and in all parts of your company, celebrate it whenever and wherever it occurs. Small-scale innovation "functions like fireflies," says Thomas. "It lights up the sky for a while, then goes away, then appears in another part of the company."

The solution isn't always close at hand.

As systems theorist Peter Senge points out, many companies become prisoners of their own success—they keep trying to do the same things that worked in the past, even though the circumstances require something different. For this reason, the solution to the problem you're facing will often come from outside your company.

Back in the early 20th century, when Dupont was wrestling with what to do when a business becomes too large for the founders to handle and when there are no more relatives to run the firm, the solution arose at General Motors, under Alfred Sloan's leadership. GM's very success, however, gave rise to the problem of the managerial corporation: How do you achieve fast growth without a highly centralized management structure? "That solution came in the 1970s, not from GM but from companies like Polaroid, Hewlett-Packard, and Digital," says Thomas. "And the problems that Polaroid faced in trying to own its entire product-development process, to be its own source of innovation, have been more successfully dealt with by a company like Cisco, which acquires innovation through purchases of innovative firms."

Look beyond the traditional boundaries of your industry when you're searching for answers. Inland found inspiration for its game-changing move in the history of oil companies such as Mobil and Exxon, which figured out how to drive their production and refining instead of having those operations drive them, and in the process turned regional businesses into international powerhouses.

Spend more time honing your ability to pull the plug than on reducing your failure rate.

Companies often build in procedures to make their R&D more productive. These steps can be useful as far as they go, but the fundamental reality, says Sutton, is that "if you want innovation, you have to be able to tolerate high failure rates." A more worthwhile use of your time may be to fine-tune your organizational ability to kill unpromising projects earlier on in the process. Some companies give their creative teams incentives to self-police. At the pharmaceutical firm Novartis, if a team trying to develop a new compound decides that it's not heading in the right direction, it gets a bonus for pulling the plug on its own project. "At various times in the creative process you need to demolish ideas—without demolishing people, of course," says Sutton, and this is where having a few pessimists on the team can prove invaluable.

"The methods for supporting routine work—the sta-bilizing and homogenizing activities that are at the heart of accepted management practice—are the worst things you can do for innovation," Sutton continues. "The only way you'll get innovation is by putting up with a lot of constructive friction and destabilization."

For Further Reading

Weird Ideas That Work: 11 1/2 Practices for Promoting, Managing, and Sustaining Innovation by Robert I. Sutton (2002, Free Press)

Reprint U0205C

Applying Innovation Strategies

• • •

Deciding where and how to generate fresh ideas is a key step in innovating. The articles in this section present a variety of strategies for catalyzing and leveraging new ideas. As you'll discover, the savviest innovators look both outside and inside their companies for inspiration.

Some automakers, for example, partner with suppliers and research outfits to stay on top of new transmission and fuel-cell technologies. Analyzing competing companies' offerings can also generate ideas. For instance, if a rival firm is providing more performance and features in its products than customers want or can use, you take advantage of the situation by building convenience into your company's products.

To spur fresh ideas within your organization, foster a culture that encourages people to take risks and learn from both successes and failures while experimenting with new ideas. And look for opportunities to combine incremental improvements to your existing products and services with bigger changes.

The New Rules of R&D

• • •

Henry Chesbrough

Not so long ago, internal research and development was viewed as a strategic asset. Companies such as DuPont, Merck, IBM, GM, and AT&T did the most research in their respective industries and earned most of the profits as well. Today, however, even though American industrial corporations as a whole spent more than $189 billion on R&D in 2002, many leading companies are dissatisfied with their R&D investments.

Why? Increasingly hard-pressed to show shareholders a return on this capital, they have cut back their R&D efforts sharply. Once-robust R&D centers like the ones at Bell Labs and GE are but shadows of their former selves. Indeed, most of the premier industrial research labs of the 20th century have retreated from their historic mission of scientific discovery.

What's more, companies are finding that many promising ideas leak out of their internal labs into the external market. Xerox's Palo Alto Research Center (PARC) managed its research lab according to the best practices of the day. But some of the most valuable ideas it created were jettisoned because they didn't fit with Xerox's copier and printer business. A handful of them eventually became hugely successful IPOs—their combined market capitalization at one point was greater than Xerox's—but Xerox reaped none of the rewards.

But it would be a grave mistake to give up on internal research. Not only can internal discoveries be a source of competitive advantage, but they can also generate valuable intellectual property and revenue streams. For example, IBM earned $1.9 billion from patent licensing and royalties in 2001, and its internal research helps it maintain the lead in the rapidly growing systems integration market.

What's needed is a more outward-facing approach to R&D. Not only should you be looking to leverage external technology in your internal R&D, you should also be identifying ways that other firms can use your technology in their businesses. This approach, which I call *open innovation,* places a new set of demands on internal R&D and changes the rules of the innovation game.

Moving Beyond
"Not Invented Here" Thinking

In the golden age of internal R&D, dismissing a product as "Not Invented Here" (NIH) signified the superiority of internally developed technology and the risks of relying on outside suppliers for important parts of your product. Back then, to develop and market a complex product effectively, it was best to do it all yourself. Companies built deep pools of internal expertise in a wide variety of areas and used them to develop all the critical elements required. This was how GM built its cars, IBM its mainframe computers, Xerox its copiers and printers, and AT&T the U.S. phone system.

Such thinking is now obsolete. Skilled people are more mobile than they used to be, and they are spreading technology and know-how to newer and smaller companies. Useful knowledge is widespread: Firms with fewer than 1,000 employees used to account for less than 5% of U.S. R&D expenditures as recently as 1981; today, they account for more than 20%. Large companies of more than 25,000 employees used to provide more than 70% of industrial R&D; today, they provide about 40%. In short, there seem to be fewer economies of scale in R&D these days. As a result, "Not Invented Here" has acquired a completely different signification. Now it means "Don't reinvent the wheel—instead, use a perfectly good wheel to build a better vehicle."

Applying Innovation Strategies

Once a company accepts the importance of accessing external technology, the focus of internal R&D changes from one of depth within a discipline to one of breadth and integration across disciplines. Whereas old-school research labs developed new technologies from the ground up, open-innovation labs must scan the external environment of universities, start-ups, competitors, and others to identify promising technology for internal use. They must also develop architectures that are capable of easily integrating these outside technologies into their complex internal systems.

Automakers, for example, don't try to reinvent the wheel anymore; they partner with suppliers and research outfits to stay on top of new transmission and fuel-cell technologies. Their in-house R&D teams focus on integrating the technologies they see emerging from their supply base. By investing in advanced computer modeling and simulation technologies, they have been able to reduce the time it takes to produce new designs and to experiment with more combinations of the myriad parts that go into a car. This expertise provides the ongoing rationale for internal R&D investment. Toyota, which buys the same parts that are available to any automaker, uses its systems integration skill to build better cars than its competitors do from those same parts.

Companies can also leverage external technologies to enhance their value chain. Merck invests in start-up companies that address inefficiencies in its drug-development process. One such company focuses on recruiting physi-

cians and their patients into clinical trials. Another focuses on automating the FDA reporting processes. Shav-
ing even a month or two off the time it takes to perform
these tasks extends the effective patent life of Merck's
drugs, which can translate into millions of dollars. Similarly, Metropolitan Life Insurance has shifted its back-
office claims processing to an outside company. The ven-
dor's newer technology and higher claims volume (from
handling other companies' claims) result in lower costs
for MetLife.

Combating the "Not Sold Here" Virus

Leveraging external technologies is only half the R&D
battle. The other half? Letting other firms put your ideas
to use. Here, you encounter the "Not Sold Here" (NSH)
virus—the business-side counterpart to the NIH virus
that infects many R&D departments.

NSH-afflicted thinking says, "If we're not selling it in
our own sales channels, we won't let anyone else sell it,
either." When your sales and marketing people insist
that they must have exclusive use of your technology and
want to restrict the technology to your company's own
channels of distribution, you know you've got an NSH
epidemic on your hands. Although it may seem rea-
sonable to give your current sales and marketing organization exclusive use of your ideas, this approach is
unlikely to deliver the most value. If a company makes a

component and then uses it in its own product, it can often reduce its costs by allowing other companies to buy that same component for their uses.

For example, the film animation studio Pixar pioneered the use of its RenderMan animation software to make its award-winning films. But Pixar also sells RenderMan to other companies, which use it for a variety of computer simulation purposes. This spreads the component's fixed costs over increased volumes. More subtly, it forces the product (the Pixar movie) to compete on its own value-added instead of relying upon exclusive access to the component (RenderMan). If the product can justify its added value, in other words, it benefits from lower-cost components. If it cannot, the component is doomed to the limited business it can realize from its captive (internal) customer.

Outright licensing can also be a means of bringing your ideas to bear on a much wider array of business opportunities. Not only can such licensing be done at little incremental cost to you, but it can also generate important incremental revenue and profit. What's more, companies that license your ideas may also need consulting help to make the best use of those ideas, thereby creating a second revenue stream alongside the initial royalty payments. By unlocking such revenue streams, you'll be able to justify your innovation investments when others are cutting back.

In a world in which knowledge and skills are widely distributed, you can no longer assume that all the best people in your field work for you. Nor can you assume that your company has a monopoly on the best technology or the best way to use ideas. Opening your innovation process to include the ideas and businesses of others is the only way to make these new realities work to your advantage.

Reprint U0305D

Performance, Convenience, Price:

What's Your Brand About?

• • •

Scott D. Anthony and Clayton M. Christensen

This past June, a front-page article in the *Wall Street Journal* describing Barnes & Noble's roll-out of a line of "store-brand" books sent shock waves through the publishing world. The Barnes & Noble effort enables consumers to purchase such classics as Melville's *Moby Dick* and Hawthorne's *The Scarlet Letter* in high-quality editions at competitively low prices—sometimes as much as 50% below what they would pay for the same book from such publishers as Bertelsmann or Penguin Books. Barnes & Noble hopes to mimic the success of supermarkets and other large retailers that have used a store-brand strategy to capture shelf space—and value—away from brand-name consumer products companies.

Should this announcement have caused such tremors? Through the lenses of our theories of strategy and innovation, the answer is—emphatically—yes. Barnes & Noble's action indicates that within the publishing arena, circumstances have changed, meaning the power to capture value from a brand will increasingly shift from book publishers such as HarperCollins and Houghton-Mifflin to the channels that stock and sell the books.

Most observers would call this development commoditization and use the word as an epithet to describe a process that results in companies being unable to profitably differentiate their products and services. Indeed, the specter of commoditization sends chills down every executive's spine—and well it should. Throughout history, competitors have figured out how to emulate even the most proprietarily differentiated products and services.

To ward off such threats, many companies invest substantial time and money building powerful brands that can carry a premium cachet and associated premium pricing for as long—and as effectively—as possible. However, the same forces that cause commoditization of products and services precipitate the commoditization of brands.

But there is another side of the commoditization coin. Almost always, the forces that cause a product or service to commoditize cause something else to decommoditize. The same is true of brands. When one set of brands ceases to carry value, another set, somewhere else in the same industry's value chain at another stage of value-added, starts to create worth.

This article presents a model that managers can use to understand the forces that can cause the erosion of brand value and to identify where in a value chain opportunities to create new brands or to revitalize existing brands can emerge.

In short, we suggest there are three different types of brands:

1. Performance brands

2. Convenience brands

3. Price brands.

Overshooting—providing more performance than customers can utilize—leads to performance brands migrating from product producers to component providers. Overshooting also creates opportunities for retailers to create convenience and price brands.

What Branding Looks Like Through the Disruptive Innovation Lens

As with many issues in strategy and innovation, the disruptive innovation model helps to visualize how and why the value of proprietary products and brands can be built and how they can erode. The model, displayed in "Branding and the disruptive innovation model," describes the tendency for the pace of technological progress to outstrip the ability of customers to utilize that progress. For purposes of this discussion, there are two important elements of the theory to highlight.

First, the theory distinguishes between two fundamental circumstances. On the left side of the diagram, the functionality of products and services is "not good enough" to meet customer demands. On the right side of the diagram, the functionality of products and services is "more than good enough" to meet customer demands.

Branding and the disruptive innovation model

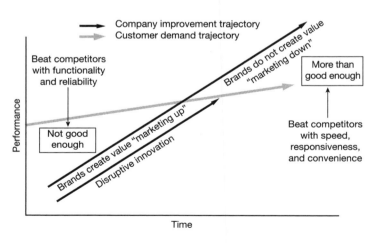

Applying Innovation Strategies

Many innovators believe that focusing on product quality and making the best possible products is the key to creating premium brands. This is true—in some circumstances. Companies can indeed build valuable performance brands around products that are not yet good enough to deliver the functionality and reliability that customers need. In other words, companies can create powerful performance brands when they are on the left side of "Branding and the disruptive innovation model"—when they are "marketing up" toward customers who want more than available products provide. A well-crafted brand can step in and close some of the gap between what customers need and what they fear they might get if they buy the product from a supplier of unknown reputation.

Levi Strauss & Co. honed the brand name of its denim jeans during a period when the durability of clothing was not good enough for rugged work. Procter & Gamble built its valuable Crest toothpaste brand in an era when few people were satisfied that their teeth could be protected from cavities. For the same reason, food brands such as Birds Eye and Green Giant vegetables, Swift Premium meats, and Kellogg's cereals emerged when the quality and consistency of factory-processed foods was highly variable and spoilage was common. These are all examples of performance brands that became established in the "not good enough" phase of industry development.

Opportunities continue to exist to create performance brands wherever performance is not good enough. For example, consider the potential for brand creation in the real estate management industry. Mentioning the name of most building management companies conjures up images of somebody who will squeeze every penny out of tenants and fix things as begrudgingly and minimally as possible. Nobody is ever oversatisfied by the trustworthiness, helpfulness, friendliness, and reliability of their landlords. This would be a great venue for establishing a brand.

When performance is not yet good enough, companies must compete by making the best products possible. Our statement that performance brands create value only in the circumstance where performance is not yet good enough, however, means that performance brands begin losing their ability to create value when performance becomes more than good enough. This leads to the second important implication of this model.

As described in *The Innovator's Dilemma* and *The Innovator's Solution,* companies innovate faster than people's lives change, so what is not good enough today becomes more than good enough tomorrow. This process is called *overshooting.* Because it creates a "more than good enough" situation, overshooting triggers the process of commoditization. If overshooting did not occur, customers would always be willing to pay for improved performance.

How can you tell when overshooting has occurred, and what are its implications? Overshot customers lose their willingness to pay premiums for improvements that they once valued; in economic parlance, they derive diminishing marginal benefits from product enhancements. Companies add extra features that never get used. People begin to complain about things they ignored in the past. "This product is too complicated," they say. "And it costs too much."

When overshooting occurs and the performance of a class of products from multiple suppliers becomes manifestly more than adequate, the brands are less able to command premium prices. Performance brands lose their ability to sustain premium prices with customers in the least-demanding market tiers, and the erosion of the brand's value then creeps upward, tier by tier. "Branding and the disruptive innovation model" illustrates this, showing that investments in performance brand building are much less likely to bear fruit when "marketing downward" to oversatisfied customers.

People often assume that once price begins to matter, then the game is over and commoditization has occurred. Part of that statement is correct. Price-based competition means that companies can no longer command premium prices for a particular type of brand.

What is bad news for some companies, however, is good news for others. Specifically, overshooting creates three brand-related opportunities (summarized in "Where branding power resides"):

Where branding power resides

"Not good enough" era	"More than good enough" era
Components	**Subsystems**
Product design and assembly	Product design and assembly
	Retailing– Convenience
Retailing	**Retailing– Price**

1. Providers of key components or subsystems that improve the critical aspects of functionality and reliability can build performance brands.

2. Retailers that make it easy for consumers to get what they want, when they want it, can build convenience brands.

3. Retailers can offer overshot customers a "good enough" product at significantly lower prices, building price brands.

Let's discuss each of these opportunities.

1. Outside-to-Inside Migration

The first important shift is the migration of performance brands from the "outside" to the "inside." In the
not-yet-good-enough circumstance on the left side of the
disruption diagram, for engineering reasons the architecture of the best-performing products usually involves
a proprietary, interdependent design. Functionality and
reliability are determined in the system design—by the
way in which the components are designed to fit and
function together. It is in this era that valuable brands
reside on the end-use product—because that is the stage
of value-added where the valuable performance is created.

When overshooting occurs, however, and improvements in speed, convenience, and customization become
the types of innovations that matter most to customers,
the architecture of most products and services tends
to become modular. Modular designs enable product assemblers to substitute subsystems without needing to
redesign entire products, and to mix and match components and subsystems from different suppliers. When
this happens—beginning, as always, at the bottom of the
market—the ability of the disruptive suppliers of modular products to move up-market to ever-more-attractive
customers is determined not at the level of the system
architecture, but by the subsystems and components
from which the product is assembled.

In other words, what is not good enough flips from

the architecture to the subsystems—from the outside to the inside. The opportunity to create valuable brands shifts as well—from the outside to the inside.

The clearest example of this shift comes from the computer industry, where, in the 1990s, the brands belonging to Intel and Microsoft Windows stole valuable branding power from IBM and Hewlett-Packard. Modular, industry-standard architectures came to dominate the mainstream business tiers of the market. At that point, the microprocessor inside and the operating system became the factors that enabled assemblers such as Dell and Compaq to move up-market. The locus of the powerful brands, therefore, migrated from what was on the box to what was in the box—those subsystems that defined the product's performance.

2. The Birth of Convenience Brands

The second important shift that results from overshooting happens at the retail level. Overshooting creates opportunities for retailers to take "good enough" products and deliver them in highly convenient, customized ways. In the process, they can create very powerful "convenience" brands that help customers get exactly what they want, exactly when they want it, as conveniently as possible.

Consider the stores that populate your local shopping mall—places like the Gap, Abercrombie & Fitch,

Williams-Sonoma, and so on. Most people have no idea who makes the products these stores sell, and most people don't really care. In fact, companies such as the Gap and Abercrombie & Fitch use contract manufacturers that make products for multiple companies. Because customers don't care how rugged clothes are—since they go out of style before they fall apart—many, many suppliers can produce "good enough" clothing. The power now resides with organizations that can supply stylish products to targeted customers and arrange those products in an engaging, attractive way. Hence, branding power has migrated from the products to the distribution channel, because the channel improves upon what is now not good enough, the customer's ability to quickly find and coordinate stylish outfits.

In other words, "category killers" are just that because they make shopping for a particular type of product so simple and convenient, allowing people to more expediently get things done. In this way, they have the opportunity to create valuable convenience brands. Stores go from a "house of brands" to a "branded house." The insight from our theories is that the process of overshooting also drives this change.

3. The Creation of Price Brands

Finally, let's take a look at companies that follow strategies similar to Barnes & Noble's and create their own store-branded products. Through our lenses, these retailers' brands are "disruptive innovations." They can't get traction in tiers of the market where customers are not yet satisfied with a product's performance. But in a more-than-good-enough situation, making the best products offers little defense for the value of premium brands. Store-branded products have the potential to build powerful price brands that erode and even topple the market positions of powerful product companies.

As always, what creates a threat to some constitutes opportunity for others. Tesco and Sainsbury's Supermarkets, the two largest food retailers in Britain, for example, have decisively wrested control of valuable brands away from consumer products giants such as Unilever and Procter & Gamble. Category by category, the retailers are driving many branded products off the shelves with their own private-label offerings. A handful of high-priced branded products remain solely to sit on the shelf and remind customers how much money they can save by buying store-branded products provided by anonymous manufacturers that are clearly capable of making good enough products. Overall, almost 40% of products sold by U.K. food retailers are private-label. In some categories, the stores' brands command a 90% market share. Canadian retailer Loblaw has been similarly successful.

The same shift is happening in the U.S. food retailing industry. Store-branded products are incrementally taking shelf space away from premium-branded products, beginning with the most basic staples. For example, currently almost a quarter of the pasta products sold in the U.S. are private label.

To consumer products companies, this is horrible news. For food retailers—and their customers—this is great news. Store brands provide similar products at lower prices, and food retailers actually earn higher margins on the lower-priced products. In a business that operates on razor-thin margins, this is very significant.

> The process of product commoditization and the diminishment of valuable brands are at work in every market, all the time.

Barnes & Noble's latest venture closely follows this pattern. Notice that Barnes & Noble presciently decided to start with "classic" books. Classics exist in the public domain—you don't need to have any special copyright protection to publish them. Most customers know exactly what they are getting when they purchase *Moby Dick*. They don't need a particular publisher's stamp of approval to tell them the book is worth reading. If history is any guide, Barnes & Noble will now move up the publishing value chain and capture increasing value from publishers.

Of course, retailers driving this change need to be careful that their own success doesn't lead them to fall into the same trap of providing too much to customers, creating opportunities for new companies to compete in new ways. We hate to say it, but because the trajectory of performance improvement almost always outstrips customers' abilities to utilize those improvements, the processes of product commoditization and the diminishment of valuable product brands are at work in every market, all the time. Indeed, in some markets, the process works its way from the bottom to the top in a matter of years. In others, it takes decades, but eventually it does happen.

We emphasize that this article isn't claiming that the formula for success that worked in the past will not work in the future and that all companies need to change if they are to succeed. As long as brands serve to close the gap between what customers need and what they can get, they will create value. But because that gap usually exists only temporarily, firms must watch for shifts in the location of opportunities to create new brands.

The process can take a long time. In some markets, it never reaches the upper tier, where customers have come to have a strong emotional connection to a particular brand-name product. But the process is never-ending, and because it is never-ending, there are never-ending opportunities to take advantage of it.

Reprint S0311A

Where Does the Competitive Advantage Lie?

• • •

Loren Gary

Michael Collins is looking to diversify. His company, Big Idea Group, currently produces only children's toys, but he thinks his process for discovering, refining, and bringing ideas to market can work in other niches.

As the Harvard Business School case "What's the BIG Idea?" explains, Collins is setting his sights on the home and garden business. Clayton Christensen, Robert and Jane Cizik Professor of Business Administration at Harvard Business School, uses this case to frame the central questions for anyone trying to understand the sources of innovation, and what blocks it, inside companies.

Does Collins have the creativity to pull this off? Focus instead on Big Idea Group's "process of innovation and value creation," says Christensen. Lack of creativity is rarely the reason for lackluster products and services coming out of the pipeline. "There's usually some process by which a potentially great idea gets prostituted into something lackluster, or by which the wrong idea gets put forward."

Break the innovative process down and analyze each component, Christensen recommends. That will help you understand "where the competitive advantages lie." His analysis highlights two stages of Big Idea Group's four-phase process of innovation: the generation of ideas and the winnowing of the ideas down to a manageable few.

The Idea-Generation Phase

Large toy manufacturers often discard the products sent to them by outside inventors without even looking at them. Because of their hurdle rate—the minimum return required on a contemplated investment—they probably don't have the time or resources to devote to smaller ideas that won't have much chance of wide distribution.

Big Idea Group, by contrast, uses a low-overhead

approach that welcomes any and all inventors. These "Big Idea Hunts," held at regular intervals around the country, allow inventors to present their ideas to a panel of industry experts. Collins's practice of giving constructive feedback on every idea, his reputation for deep knowledge, and the impressive industry contacts he's acquired have earned him a loyal following: his idea-generation process yields 200 interesting concepts a month.

The Winnowing Phase

The large toy manufacturers say they're starved for imaginative ideas and have been struggling for years to develop new products that don't rely on movie tie-ins. How can this be? "Inside the large manufacturers you've got middle managers who want to put forward only those products that look like what's been approved in the past," explains Christensen. A product idea that gets rejected or that gets approved and then bombs will damage the middle manager's career. "As a consequence of this natural process of deciding what to carry forward, the ideas that get developed into business plans are the ones that look a lot like the ideas that got funded before."

"This is not necessarily a bad process," says Christensen, "it's just good at certain things." For example, after Sony's founder Akio Morita stepped away from the business in the early 1980s, the company's marketing group hired its first MBAs, who brought with them a data-driven analytical approach to understanding new market opportunities. "That's a great process for finding gaps in well-established markets," says Christensen, "but it's a bad process for making intuitive bets."

Relying largely on Morita's intuition, Sony had a string of "12 bona fide disruptive technologies that created new markets with new customers and then killed off the market leaders" between 1950 and 1979. The analytical approach, by contrast, produced significant innovations during the 1980s and 1990s, but they were all "late entrants into well-established markets."

What kinds of products are best suited for analytical thinking and what kinds are best suited for intuitive thinking? "If you can understand how and why a process does what it does," Christensen concludes, "when an idea comes into the pipeline, you'll know how to use your process—or whether to circumvent it and create a parallel process for developing the idea."

Reprint U0207F

Innovation Inside

• • •

Judith A. Ross

Inside a Whirlpool Corporation manufacturing plant, a group of employees including a line worker and an engineer were talking about tailgate parties. Wouldn't it be great, they fantasized, if you could pour drinks and refrigerate and cook food out of the back of a car—all while playing your favorite music?

The result of this discussion? Whirlpool's Gator Pak, a product now in development that will allow consumers to create customized tailgating devices with a range of options—grills, cooling and warming drawers, beverage taps, microwave ovens, and sound systems. The Gator Pak is one of a host of new company innovations, including an in-sink dishwasher, a cooking range with refrigeration capabilities, and a line of personal appliances targeting 18- to 34-year-olds. The ideas for these products all stem from the same source: a large-scale

Whirlpool change initiative that has driven a commitment to innovation throughout the company and made it an organizational competency.

Because relatively few companies have achieved sustainable innovation over time, many experts have advised firms to seek innovation from the outside. The idea here is that companies should focus on their core competencies—manufacturing, branding, distribution, or what have you—while finding the new ideas they need for future growth through acquisitions and partnerships.

> New ideas pressure-test corporate strategy and add to the variety of alternatives available to an organization.

This model has proved successful for many organizations, even those with strong innovation track records. Procter & Gamble CEO A.G. Lafley recently told shareholders, "Our vision is that 50% of all P&G discovery and invention could come from outside the company."

But other companies are eschewing external investment to focus instead on developing a culture and internal processes that unleash the power of ideas within their own organization. The energy and commitment to innovation driven through these firms have yielded some promising new products. Just as important, the emergence of each new idea pressure-tests corporate strategy and adds to the variety of alternatives available to the organization. And this goes to the heart of building organizational resilience.

"Resilience depends on variety," write Gary Hamel, visiting professor of strategy and international management at London Business School and director of the Woodside Institute, and Liisa Välikangas, a senior research fellow at the Woodside Institute, in the *Harvard Business Review*. "The larger the variety of actions available to a system, the larger the variety of perturbations it is able to accommodate." By relying on internal capabilities to produce the strategic variety your company needs, you further reduce the likelihood that you will be a victim of outside turbulence.

Several core elements are key to building sustainable commitments to innovation inside a company. Among them are a shared mental model of commitment, the availability of internal seed money, structures that encourage experimentation and tolerate failure, and the ability to measure innovation's value.

From a Vision to an Embedded Model

Whirlpool's change program was launched in 1999 to release the company from a commodity-based industry and transform it into one that innovates across all the customer touch points. The charge to implement the organization's new vision, "Innovation from everyone and everywhere," was led quite visibly by CEO David R. Whitwam, who worked to cascade a shared commitment to innovation throughout the organization.

Whitwam began by working with his leadership team to create a shared mental model of embedment that would give innovation deep roots in the organization. They achieved this through a visual framework the company calls an embedment wheel. Its outermost layer depicts vision and goals. The middle layer outlines the infrastructure required to support embedment of innovation at every level of the organization, and encompasses leadership accountability and development, culture and values, financial and human resources, incentives and systems for alignment, knowledge management and learning, and measurement and reporting. The center of this visual tool contains the actual processes and tools needed to innovate.

Nancy Tennant Snyder, corporate vice president of strategic competency creation and leadership, says she had learned from previous change efforts at Whirlpool that all these elements had to be acted upon simultaneously. "We needed to fire on all cylinders to make the change. We couldn't just send people to training or change the compensation system. We had to do all of it as an infrastructure, and it all had to move forward together."

Putting the Company's Money Where Its Mouth Is

While moving on many fronts simultaneously is critical in a shift like the one Whirlpool undertook, says Deborah L. Duarte, a consultant and coauthor, with Snyder, of *Strategic Innovation: Embedding Innovation as a Core Competency in Your Organization,* some aspects of this type of program may be more visible early on than others. In Whirlpool's case it was the seed funds. These are small amounts of money, $25,000 to $100,000, set aside for small experiments around one aspect of an innovation and disbursed by middle managers, boards of managers, and internal innovation consultants. To request the funds, applicants submit a business plan describing the innovation as a business idea; the process eliminates the need to jump through several hierarchical hoops to get the money.

Says Duarte, "A change strategy must be robust, using all of the elements if you are to show the workforce you mean business. On the other hand, if you can find some sort of quick win that will have impact and is easy to do, let it get out ahead. The seed money showed the seriousness of the effort—the trick was to also highlight the rest of the program."

Embracing Experimentation— and Failure

Small, iterative experiments, like the ones funded at Whirlpool, are the lifeblood of innovation, says Harvard Business School professor Stefan Thomke, author of *Experimentation Matters: Unlocking the Potential of New Technologies for Innovation.* Experimentation can help firms manage technical, production, and marketplace uncertainties. "Companies don't experiment enough—or well enough. They hire lots of outsiders and try to draw on their experience. Why not go to experimentation? Quite often you can resolve questions at a fraction of the cost of other methods." The challenge, he cautions, lies in fostering a willingness to learn from both success and failure. "Failures are inevitable. You have to have a lot of failure in process to achieve success in outcome. Experiments should be designed to maximize the information and insights they produce. Especially in the early stages it is important not to delay things in order to prevent failure. An approach of rapid iterations allows you to learn quickly from both success and failure, and drive that learning down."

There is also the issue of arithmetic, write Hamel and Välikangas. "It takes thousands of ideas to produce dozens of promising stratlets to yield a few outsize successes. Yet only a handful of companies have committed themselves to broad-based, small-scale strategic experimentation."

A willingness to learn from experimentation—and hence failure—signals a huge cultural shift for most organizations. "Tolerance to well-intentioned mistakes is crucial to the innovation process," says Chad Mellen, vice president of marketing for luggage maker Tumi, a company with a long-held commitment to internal innovation.

Whirlpool has made a concerted effort to help its workforce take innovative risks, and its senior leaders have spoken publicly about learning from failure. They have even rewarded it. "One of the high-profile individuals who started an innovation and ran it for some time before it was shelved not only speaks highly of his innovation experience but is now in a significant job," Snyder says. The ideas that don't succeed the first time around are referred to as "shelved," Snyder says, "to connote that they are not dead or valueless." In fact, a new step added to all Whirlpool innovations requires that teams look through shelved ideas, highlighting them as an asset. And Whirlpool India routinely reviews them to see if any would be applicable in their marketplace.

Practices That Sustain and Measure

Several organizational commitments at Tumi have allowed it to sustain an internal innovation competency for several decades. The first is the ability to build rapidly on existing products or concepts. The firm reviews and updates its product line on a seasonal basis. The high frequency allows Tumi designers to keep pace with a fast-changing market. For example, this process might expose the need in one of the collections for a bag that will hold a new large-screen laptop recently brought to market.

Next, the firm recognizes and encourages the ad hoc nature of creativity by building time into its design cycles for designers to pursue new concepts of their own inspiration.

Finally, in spite of its organizational commitment to internal innovation, Tumi seeks outside inspiration. For example, the design department holds regular meetings to discuss possible carryovers from other industries, casting a wide net in its pursuit of best practices in product design and functionality. Intent on extending its reach to consumers desiring a forward-looking product, Tumi recently launched a product line inspired in part by the breakthrough styling of the Audi TT sports car, says designer and vice president Timm Fenton. Tumi's tracer program, a customer service innovation that assigns every bag a serial number so if lost it can be returned to its owner through a central registry, was inspired by a key chain made by Tiffany that if found can be dropped in any mailbox to be returned to its owner.

All these sources of innovation are discussed and tracked in monthly meetings of Tumi's innovation committee, where new ideas are brought to the table and reviewed against business strategy. The committee comprises the company president and the heads of sales, marketing, design, and merchandising. Tumi has also embedded innovation in its sales plans, budgeting a specified amount of income to come in from new products.

As it has institutionalized its own commitment to innovation, Whirlpool has developed metrics to help gauge innovation's effectiveness. The first step in this process was for Whirlpool's leadership team to define measurable embedment goals—as opposed to results goals. Results goals are tied to the long-term business outcomes for innovation. Embedment goals focus on progress around the activities delineated on the embedment wheel. These kinds of goals required a whole new set of measures—for example, the number of key barriers removed to allow innovation to thrive or the number of jobs changed due to innovation. Senior Whirlpool executives now employ "an innovation dashboard," write Hamel and Välikangas, "that tracks the number of ideas moving through the pipeline, the percentage of those ideas that are truly new, and the potential financial impact of each one."

Even with the right vision and the right plan, a culture shift that puts innovation at a company's core for the first time is no easy sell. Simply changing the organization's mindset around failure can be a Herculean task. But as a result of the effort at Whirlpool, Snyder is convinced that with leadership support, the commitment to innovation can insinuate itself into every corner of an organization. "Look at those guys sitting around talking about tailgating who said, 'What if?'" she says. "Lo and behold, there was a mechanism there to help them. It's amazing the kind of positive energy this process unleashes."

Reprint U0401B

Is Risk the Cost of Innovation?

• • •

Hal Plotkin

Marketplaces change at blinding speed, and competitive advantage can be quickly lost. You need your employees to think innovatively, but you don't want to encourage dumb mistakes or bad business decisions. Experienced managers say the best way to draw the line is to combine a clearly stated policy that anticipates mistakes with a program that conspicuously rewards workers who succeed.

For example, Mark Rohney, president of UPS e-Ventures, goes well beyond the usual mantra of encouraging smart failure—he celebrates it, within strict limits. It's part of your job as a leader, Rohney says, to let employees know that you expect failures to happen sometimes. "To be a success in my eyes, it doesn't necessarily have to mean that you built a business. You're just as successful if you kill one. I spend a lot of time with my project teams and my senior management, telling them, 'It's OK to be wrong. It's OK that it's a bad idea.'"

One manager who takes that approach is George Zimmer, the founder and CEO of the Men's Wearhouse. Since its founding in 1973, it has grown from a single store in Houston to a 680-outlet firm that now controls 15% of the U.S. market for tailored men's clothes. Many of Zimmer's best customer-service practices have come from his workers. Zimmer's employees have been known to rush freshly tailored suits to departing executives at airports and entertain children while their parents shop.

Zimmer says creating a corporate culture where employees are willing to take the risks inherent in trying out new approaches would have been impossible if his workers didn't feel free to make up their own rules from time to time. A policy of forgiving mistakes has to be more than just words if managers want to get the best performance from their people. Zimmer's been willing to take that philosophy all the way to its outer limits to reinforce the point.

After an employee confessed to stealing $3,000 from the till to feed a compulsive gambling habit, Zimmer overruled objections from the employee's direct supervisor and let the worker keep his job while making restitution through paycheck deductions. Experts had advised Zimmer that the thief would probably steal again (he did, and was later fired). But Zimmer says losing the money was a small price to pay for preserving a winning company culture.

Tell employees what they should do, not just what they shouldn't.

Managers can often reinforce employees' understanding of risk-taking boundaries through their own actions. Some firms also find it useful to provide written guidelines about exactly what constitutes unacceptable behavior. What helps most is to provide regular, eye-catching examples of the type of risks employees *should* be taking. Men's Wearhouse, for example, layers its mistake-tolerating management approach with a heavily promoted companywide incentive program called "Go the Extra Mile" that is designed to get employees experimenting with ideas that have never been tried before.

The program facilitates the development and transfer of the best of those practices by giving away an extra week of vacation once per quarter. Every nominee receives an Extra Mile T-shirt simply for having his or her name submitted. "It's had a huge impact on our organization," says Zimmer. "And all we're really doing is giving away four weeks of vacation and some T-shirts."

Use the milestone approach to minimize financial risks.

When it comes to risk taking in business, however, the trickiest issues often involve financial decisions, such as whether to undertake a costly new marketing campaign or product development effort. Guy Kawasaki, CEO of Garage Technology Ventures, recommends that managers use the "milestone approach" in such circumstances. Employees should be told to break down any big, financially risky idea into phases that can be implemented in building-block fashion to test the validity of their assumptions.

"Someone might have an idea that will cost $10 million," he says, "but if you spend $200,000 on the prototype first, then see how you're doing, and stop and measure each step along the way, you can minimize the risks associated with a failure. You'll still have failures. But they'll be smaller, and they'll be just as good as learning experiences. In fact, they'll be better, because the company will still be around."

When it comes to taking risks, Kawasaki says the single best instruction managers can provide to employees is to make it clear that they are expected to treat the company's money and reputation as if they were their own and to let them know that calculated risks and mistakes won't be fatal to their careers—as long as they're innovating on behalf of customers. Then, he adds, act as if you really mean it.

Reprint C0204D

Ambidextrous Innovation

• • •

Loren Gary

Back in the 1960s, the Japanese firm Hattori-Seiko was a small player in the global watch industry. But as Michael L. Tushman and Charles A. O'Reilly III relate in *Winning Through Innovation,* Seiko made a bet on quartz technology—a low-cost alternative to mechanical movement, then the dominant technology—and transformed itself "from merely a mechanical watch firm into a quartz and mechanical watch company."

That move helped reshape the business: As quartz technology became the industry standard, Seiko and other Japanese firms prospered while the Swiss firms suffered. "By 1980, SSIH, the largest Swiss watch firm, was less than half the size of Seiko," Tushman and O'Reilly write.

The Seiko story corroborates the conclusions of population ecologists Michael Hannan and Glenn Carroll, who point to similarities between the way that organizations evolve and the punctuated equilibrium that, according to one theory, describes biological evolution. For life forms and organizations alike, write Tushman and O'Reilly, the pattern is one of "long periods of incremental change punctuated by revolutionary, or discontinuous, change." Companies that adapt their strategy and organization to suit a particular market or competitive environment will prosper. But when a major discontinuity occurs, managers are faced with "the challenge of reconstituting their organizations to adjust to the new environment. Managers who try to adapt to discontinuities by making only incremental change are unlikely to succeed."

But with the American economy in one of the longest downturns since the Great Depression, many companies are so focused on maintaining short-term profitability that they've lost sight of the need to plan for long-term growth. Concentrating on incremental improvements that will provide an immediate boost to the bottom line, they've all but forgotten to be on the lookout for improvements that can revolutionize a market or industry.

But choosing just one form of innovation won't suffice, Tushman and O'Reilly insist. To be successful, your company must be "ambidextrous," capable of managing different *innovation streams:* On the one hand, the *incremental innovations* that make a company more competitive in the short term by improving its efficiency; and, on the other, the *architectural innovations* (which reconfigure existing technology) and *discontinuous innovations* (which involve new operating principles in core subsystems or revolutionary process innovation) that ensure a company's long-term success.

The Threat of the Incremental

Some experts believe that companies' shortcomings when it comes to innovation stem from not enough deviant or outside-the-box thinking. In fact, most well-established, legacy companies have far more of that than they realize. Other experts argue that companies aren't deliberate enough in their approach to innovation, waiting around for the next big idea instead of setting up systems and processes to help them bring innovative ideas to market. But at least as far as incremental innovation is concerned, the leading companies do a pretty comprehensive job of planning.

"Taking a portfolio approach, leading companies look not just at the products in the development phase, but also at those ones in the currently-in-market phase, as well as those at the end stage of the product life cycle,"

107

says Bob Gill, president of the Product Development & Management Association. "That way, they can get a better idea of what their expected revenue targets from existing lines will be and thereby determine how much growth they're going to need from innovation. They're also very targeted in their approach to identifying new product opportunities. They look at the gaps in their product lines, their core competencies, the markets and technologies in which they excel, and the state of current markets—which are saturated, which are growing—to find the optimal arenas for innovation."

The real problem, say Tushman and O'Reilly, is not a lack of systems and processes; it's the tendency of incremental processes to strangle discontinuous and architectural ideas. Discontinuous ideas require separate and distinct processes from those used to bring incremental ideas to market. The challenge, therefore, lies in determining whether an idea has either nonincremental (that is, discontinuous or architectural) potential or incremental potential and then housing it in the appropriate process—one that will enable it to see the light of day.

But herein lies a big problem: The culture of incremental innovation often creates an institutional hostility toward the culture of architectural and discontinuous innovation. The very organizational alignment that creates short-term success often leads to a structural inertia that impairs a company's ability to change and adapt quickly. In fact, architectural and discontinuous innovation streams are so different from incremental streams that some leading experts have recommended that they be spun off into separate organizations.

But the common wisdom seems to be shifting. If you can distinguish incremental ideas from nonincremental ones and create separate tracks for shaping and developing them, then having the same management team oversee both streams—despite the "multiple, internally inconsistent architectures, competencies, and cultures"

> Running all the innovation streams out of the same organizational structure allows you to leverage your customers, technology, and infrastructure.

that will be required—has distinct advantages over spinning off the nonincremental streams and having them overseen by a different group. Not only does it become possible to do your job, improve your job, and revolutionize your job all within the same organizational structure, but the opportunities for one innovation stream to cross-pollinate the other also improve.

Multiple Innovation Streams,
One Structure

Ciba Vision, which in 1981 became the 27th entrant into the U.S. contact lens market, had by 1995 become a 6,000-person company jostling for global leadership of both the contact lens/lens care and the ophthalmics (drugs related to vision and eye health) markets. Under CEO Glen Bradley's leadership, the company realized that its current products would not be sufficient to sustain market leadership. Ciba Vision's response was to defend its position in the markets for conventional soft lenses and lens care products by investing in incremental product and process improvements and, at the same time, use the profits from these improvements to fund three autonomous teams working on discontinuous product and process innovations that had the potential to substitute for the company's current offerings.

In the contact lens market, one team worked on "an entirely new continuous production process to radically reduce the cost of manufacturing disposable soft lenses," write Tushman and O'Reilly. Another worked on "an entirely new type of contact lens that could be worn safely all day and night." The teams—made up of people from the R&D, clinical and regulatory, engineering, manufacturing, marketing, and finance areas— were "co-located, headed by strong project leaders, and allowed to work independently from the rest of the organization." Similarly, in the ophthalmics market, a team set to work developing a discontinuous pharmaceutical product named Visudyne that, in concert with laser therapy, would counteract age-related macular degeneration.

Although these teams were given a great deal of independence, a single group of managers—Bradley and his senior team—oversaw all the work. Keeping the discontinuous experimentation in one organizational structure, explains Tushman in a recent interview, enabled Ciba Vision to leverage its existing customer base. For example, had the extended wear lenses and the cheaper disposables been housed in a spinoff organization, that new firm would have had a harder time getting access to the same customers Ciba Vision already had close relationships with.

Running both processes out of the same organizational structure allows you "to leverage not just your customers, but also your technology and infrastructure" to an extent that wouldn't be possible if you had spun the nonincremental idea off into a separate organization, Tushman continues. In fact, as long as your management team is able to differentiate incremental ideas from nonincremental ones and put them into separate development tracks, "the only time you should spin off the nonincremental innovation is when there's nothing to leverage."

Cross-Pollination Benefits

Another advantage of housing incremental and nonincremental innovation streams within the same organizational structure has to do with the often unpredictable nature of innovation itself.

"The solution to the problem you're trying to solve often lies at the edge of the dominant model, or way of thinking about the problem," says Robert J. Thomas, senior research fellow at Accenture's Institute for Strategic Change. "A game-changing idea rarely shows up at the precise time it's needed—it often shows up before the problem manifests itself. So you have to have your eyes on the central tendency while allowing your peripheral vision to notice things that are relevant to your business." Thus, the chances of the incremental stream's informing the nonincremental one, and vice versa, improve when you have one team managing both processes.

An example of this cross-pollination is Cabot, a commodity chemical company that had become "culturally allergic to innovation," says Thomas. Under CEO Sam Bodman's leadership, Cabot began using advanced computer simulation methods in the mid-1990s to experiment with producing molecules of different sizes and granularity in its existing facilities, which were designed to produce only one size and granularity. Although this experimentation initially involved incremental innovation—squeezing as much as possible out of the existing technology—it led to discoveries that opened the door to nonincremental possibilities.

For instance, Cabot realized that tantalum, one of the elements it had been using to make reinforcing material for rubber products, had some remarkable properties: It was lightweight, had surprising tensile strength, was resistant to heat, and was well suited to miniaturization. As management thought about other possible uses for this element, it realized that tantalum could be a cheaper substitute for the silicon used in printed circuit boards and ultimately launched an effort to pursue microelectronic applications.

The Tensions That Crop Up

The advantages of ambidextrous innovation are not easily won. Even a small start-up like software firm Vindigo feels the tension between its processes for managing the company's legacy products (applications for personal digital assistants) and those for managing future-oriented products (applications for wireless phones). "Tensions between the incremental and the revolutionary cultures will crop up," says Vindigo CEO and President Jason Devitt. "For example, the incremental approach to market testing, which says that you add a new feature only after having gone out to your customer base to see if they want it, runs counter to the way you approach a disruptive product, which you can't test. But these tensions are minimized by our scale—with only 35 employees, it's still possible to have everyone touching all our products." Engineers, marketers, and business development people alike all switch back and forth between incremental and revolutionary projects.

> The senior team must be able to deal consistently with the inconsistencies among the innovation streams.

For established corporations, however, the tensions are magnified. Most large organizations tend to excel at either the incremental or the revolutionary form of innovation, but not both, says Accenture's Thomas. Within the pharmaceutical industry, for example, Johnson & Johnson, with its decentralized structure and highly commercial focus, tends to have a better record in incremental innovation, Thomas continues. "But Merck, with its centralized structure and academic, peer-review process for evaluating ideas, has a better record in break-through innovation. Although Merck has trouble doing things quickly, its peer review process enables lots of people to bring their knowledge to bear on a problem. Consequently, Merck is good at putting together ideas that have not been linked before, whereas at J&J, people are less likely to know what's going on in another part of the organization."

The senior teams that manage the markedly different cultures and competencies that incremental and non-incremental innovation require must function like jugglers, keeping several balls in the air at once. Their challenge, Tushman and O'Reilly write, is "to create co-existing highly differentiated and highly integrated organizations." Differentiating the units is fairly easy. Achieving the integration is not; to pull it off you need four key elements:

- A CLEAR, EMOTIONALLY ENGAGING, AND CONSISTENT VISION. The ability to appeal to a few common values helps you provide motivation and direction to multiple organizational architectures "without sounding confused or, worse, hypocritical," Tushman and O'Reilly write. At Ciba Vision, the leadership "built a bridge between the exploratory and the exploitative innovation streams by constantly hearkening back to the overarching mission of helping people maintain healthy eyes for life," Tushman says.

- A SENIOR TEAM WITH DIVERSE COMPETENCIES.
  "To deal with the diverse needs of ambidextrous organizations, it is helpful for executive teams to be homogeneous and heterogeneous," the authors continue. "When teams are relatively similar with respect to service, misunderstandings and inconsistent assumptions are reduced. But this homogeneity needs to be balanced by heterogeneity with respect to background and perspective."

- A FEW SIMPLE CORE VALUES THAT SPAN ALL THE INNOVATION STREAMS. When *USA Today* created usatoday.com to provide instantaneous news, the print reporters were upset that their stories would be scooped by the dot-com. But a commitment to the values of fairness, accuracy, and trust in both groups helped President and Publisher Tom Curley overcome these tensions, says Tushman.

- A COMMON-FATE REWARD SYSTEM FOR ALL SENIOR TEAM MEMBERS. This helps "ensure that team members will work to balance the exploitation and the exploration, treat them as two simultaneously necessary elements instead of tradeoffs," says Tushman.

"A senior team that gets it," concludes Tushman, "is one that understands the need for the divergent processes and is able to deal consistently with the inconsistencies—that is, to embrace the inherent contradictions between winning in the short term and innovation for the long term."

For Further Reading

Winning Through Innovation: A Practical Guide to Leading Organizational Change and Renewal by Michael L. Tushman and Charles A. O'Reilly III (2002, Harvard Business School Press)

Reprint U0304B

Testing an Idea's Potential

• • •

Once you've generated some promising-sounding ideas, you need to gauge which of them are most likely to score successes in the marketplace (if they're products or services) and which stand the best chance of generating the efficiencies your company is looking for (if they're process innovations). The articles in this section provide helpful guidelines.

For instance, you'll read about specific criteria a new offering must meet in order to succeed in the marketplace—such as being easy to buy and use and providing greater benefits than rival offerings. You'll also learn how to extract maximum value from your idea-testing budget; for instance, by inviting consumers to engage with a product sketch or prototype, so you get the most accurate feedback. And you'll find suggestions for refining your high-potential idea based on feedback you gather. Finally, you'll discover suggestions for anticipating—and counteracting—competitors' potential responses to your new idea.

Can You Spot
the Sure Winner?

· · ·

Eric Mankin

In August 2003, Johnson & Johnson received approval from the U.S. Food and Drug Administration to sell the Independence iBOT 3000 Mobility System, an electronic wheelchair developed in partnership with Dean Kamen, the inventor of the Segway Human Transporter. At its introduction, the wheelchair received a lot of press because it can do things conventional wheelchairs can't: it can climb stairs; it can move over uneven terrain and climb curbs; and it can extend upward, bringing the user to eye level with someone standing.

These features were impressive and unprecedented when the iBOT was unveiled almost a year ago. Johnson

& Johnson invested eight years and $150 million to bring the iBOT to market, and created a new company, Independence Technology, to drive sales.

Was the investment worth it? The headlines may say yes, but do they tell the whole story? Through work I've done since 2001 researching the promises and prospects of innovative products and services, I've developed a set of four benchmarks that can help companies evaluate and improve the probability of success for their new offerings. Measured against these criteria, the iBOT looks to face a rocky future. Using this framework can help you forecast the future of products or services that you may be developing.

Mapping a Product's Advantages

My approach compares a product or service with what's currently available. The result is a map of the product's comparative advantage in the market. The genesis of this work lies in the jobs framework developed by Clayton Christensen. The central idea of this concept is that "when a consumer buys a product, they are really 'hiring' it to get a job done. Companies are successful when they make it easier for their customers to get done what they were already trying to do," says Christensen.

In other words, a new product or service will be successful if it does a better job than existing products at satisfying the needs of a targeted customer group. But "doing a better job" actually has four dimensions. If a new product or service can exceed existing offerings across all four of these dimensions at once, then we can *guarantee* that the targeted customer group will purchase it.

The four dimensions fall into two categories, purchase motivators and purchase barriers. The new product has to excel at:

1. Providing high purchase motivators

    A. It must be less expensive than existing products (lower price).

    B. It must provide better features than existing products (greater benefits).

2. Eliminating purchase barriers

    A. It must not have any switching or adoption costs (easy to use).

    B. It must be readily available (easy to buy).

Customers for whom all four conditions apply will purchase the product or service because there are only benefits and no barriers. The closer any new product comes to succeeding in all four dimensions, the greater the chance that the product will be a winner. And, of course, the innovation will be a financial success if these

A sure winner

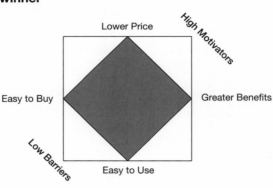

conditions can be met at a profit. The figure above ("A sure winner") illustrates the graphic representation of a sure winner.

In reality, it's a very rare new product that excels in all four dimensions simultaneously. Sometimes, however, a company manages to create something that comes awfully close.

SpinBrush: A Clear Winner

Procter & Gamble (P&G) began marketing the Crest SpinBrush line of inexpensive electric toothbrushes in 2001. By 2002, the SpinBrush was the best-selling electric toothbrush in the United States. The product's market share grew in less than 24 months to generate more than $200 million in annual sales for P&G.

The four-dimension model makes it easy to see the attraction of the SpinBrush compared with other electric toothbrushes. Price was the primary motivator for purchase. While competitive toothbrushes retailed for more than $50, the SpinBrush was designed to sell for upward of $5, depending on the model. What's more, many customers found that the SpinBrush delivered better performance. For example, since the product runs on disposable batteries, it is more portable than most electric toothbrushes.

P&G's strong distribution capabilities made the product easy to buy, as did a "try it" feature built into the packaging—shoppers could test the battery and see the brush in action at the store. Its straightforward design and reliance upon battery power made the toothbrush easier to use than its competitors.

With this kind of profile, the product had a very high probability for market success. Market research supported the predictions of the four-dimension model. The entrepreneurs who first developed the SpinBrush— then sold the company and the product to P&G—ran a test market at Meijer, a Midwest discount chain, where SpinBrush outsold the leading manual toothbrush by a factor of nearly three to one. When P&G tested the product in focus groups, participants raved about it. (See "SpinBrush.")

SpinBrush's success is not surprising. If you can launch a product that excels in all four dimensions of this model, you will have a winner.

SpinBrush

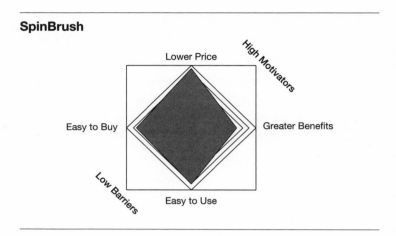

Specifications and Limitations

As a rule, the motivators (low price and greater benefits) are more important than the barriers (easy to buy and easy to use). A necessary, though not sufficient, condition of success is that a product excels along at least one of the two motivator dimensions. For instance, many products providing superior performance are successful despite being more expensive than other offerings on the market.

However, even if it excels in one or both motivators, a product or service may not be successful because there may still be high barriers to usage. One thing is certain: a product or service will not succeed if its performance is worse than existing offerings and its price is higher.

A final point: many products and services have succeeded by excelling in only one dimension. In these cases, the dimension is one of the two purchase motivators.

As with any approach to improving the market success of new products and services, the four-dimension model has its benefits as well as its limitations. Among its benefits:

1. It can scale with available data. The framework can be used with qualitative or quantitative data and is effective at varying levels of rigor.

2. It provides a basis for clarifying product intent. The framework can serve as a mechanism for ensuring agreement on the product system's intent and design.

3. It enables straightforward comparisons across differing products and markets. The history of these evaluations can serve as a mechanism for systematically improving product and service success within a business as well.

Without a doubt, the greatest limitation to this approach is that it does not address the business model underlying the new offering. Nevertheless, if the metrics indicate that you've got a promising product, you'll at least know what your next big challenge will be.

Upromise

All of the above illustrates why Upromise, an affinity investing service that contributes a small percentage of a member's purchases to a college education fund, may well succeed as a service because it addresses three crucial customer needs, though it may fail as a business if it has to build a direct sales force.

As you can see in the four-dimensional model, the product performed well along three of the four dimensions of the framework. (See "Upromise.")

However, the service is somewhat cumbersome to buy. You have to register your credit cards and grocery cards on Upromise's Web site and then open a 529 college savings account. Because there are multiple ways to earn

Upromise

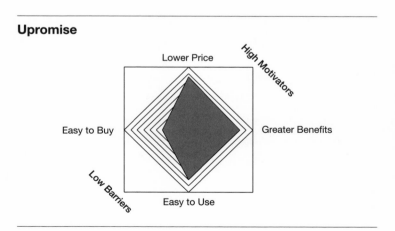

money, getting the most out of Upromise requires close attention to detail.

This is a complex process, and one of the insights gained by using the four-dimension model is that Upromise, to improve its chances of success, needs to make its service easier to buy. Commissioning a sales force to help potential customers sign up for the service would enhance the service's performance along this dimension. Its business model, however, probably cannot support the added cost of a human sales force.

With an understanding of the framework's parameters, I've found the four-dimension model to be a useful tool both for designing products and for predicting how successful the products will be. Let's return to the example discussed at the outset to see what insights the benchmarking process can provide.

J&J's iBOT 3000: Great Benefits, High Barriers

Currently, the iBOT 3000 yields the wrong answer to three of the four questions in the framework. While it may serve as a pioneering product for later extension, its current prospects are bleak.

1. The iBOT's price is more than 10 times higher than the price of existing products. The iBOT is currently priced at $29,000. A state-of-the-art

One-Dimensional Excellence: Palm

In 1996, when the first PalmPilot models were introduced, sales were less than $50 million. By June 2000, sales reached $1 billion, and the personal digital assistant (PDA) product category had been born.

The early PDAs did not score well on the four-dimension model. While the devices provided a number of features that were not available in the market (such as the ability to sync with a computer), they did so at prices that were more than 10 times higher than the paper-based organizers they were replacing.

Further, the devices had high barriers to adoption.

- They were difficult to use—entering data directly into a PalmPilot required the user to learn a new handwriting recognition system called Graffiti.
- Syncing the PDA with a computer was—and in newer versions still is—problematic, as the PDA's software often did not mesh with the computer's e-mail software (as any user of Lotus Notes will attest).
- While the devices were widely available, they were not particularly easy to buy. Companies who want to make a product or service easy to buy will often provide trial periods, for example, or bundle a set of products together (as Intuit does with its Quicken and TurboTax programs).

The PalmPilot has the following profile in the four-dimension model (see "PalmPilot"):

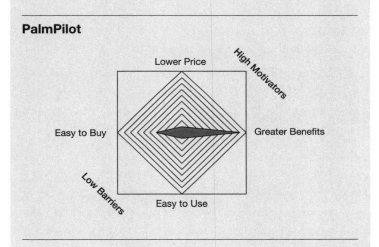

PalmPilot

Even with such a poor profile, the product became a huge success, pioneering the PDA category.

There are numerous new products that have profiles similar to the original PalmPilot, such as Gillette's new battery-powered vibrating razor, the M3 Power Razor. These types of products promise higher performance at a higher price and require training before users can get any benefits. Occasionally (as with the Palm), these products become winners. More often, they cannot overcome the barriers to success that have been built into their design.

iBOT 3000

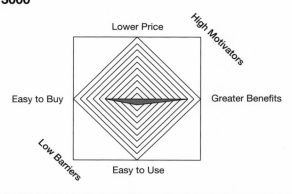

powered wheelchair costs anywhere from $1,600 to $7,500. Insurance companies' existing policies will be a major barrier to purchase. (See "iBOT 3000.")

2. The iBOT's benefits are significant, but they come with tradeoffs. One of the early product testers, Dr. Rich Barbara, found himself yearning for his conventional wheelchair. Given the iBOT for a short trial in 2001, he told the *New York Times,* "I was glad when my two weeks were up." His reason: While the iBOT can do things that conventional wheelchairs can't, it also can't do things that conventional wheelchairs can. For example, it can't fit into a small car, and it takes up more

space when in use. These drawbacks will serve to limit iBOT's market further, to those with large cars and enough space to accommodate it.

3. Switching costs are high. Users need training, and not all existing wheelchair users can use the iBOT. Since the iBOT requires the use of one hand to operate the chair by manipulating a joystick, doctors can prescribe it only to patients who pass a physical and cognitive test.

4. Current availability is limited. We can anticipate widespread availability, given Johnson & Johnson's strong distribution systems, but not immediately. The company is currently rolling it out in 10 clinics across the United States.

All major new innovation is a challenge. Based solely on probability, an innovation's chances of success are less than one in 10. The simple framework I've discussed here is useful in two ways: in evaluating the potential success of a new product or service at an early stage in its development, and in identifying areas where the new product or service can improve to increase its chances of being a winner.

Reprint S0407A

How to Place
Your Best Bets

• • •

Scott D. Anthony, Mark W. Johnson, and Matt Eyring

You have three potential innovations, all promising. But you have the resources to develop only one. Which do you choose?

Would-be innovators know that one of their biggest challenges is systematically identifying the innovations with the greatest likelihood of creating disruptive growth. Pick the wrong one, and squander a year or more of focus and investment.

The good news is that it doesn't have to be the luck of the draw anymore. By conducting a series of diagnostics, companies in any industry can quickly identify the most promising opportunities. This article shows how to conduct customer, portfolio, and competitor diagnostics to pinpoint the highest-potential opportunities and the best business models for bringing them to market. (See "Disruptive diagnostics" for the key tasks performed in each diagnostic.)

Though this article presents the three diagnostics linearly, they are rarely conducted in a linear fashion. Teams or individuals searching for disruptive opportunities can start with any of them. The results of one diagnostic will often cause an innovator to go back and revisit another. But the goal remains the same: find the option that can set your company on the path to disruptive growth.

Disruptive diagnostics

Customer Diagnostic

- Identify current and potential markets/segments

- Look for signs that markets are "disruptable" (particularly overserved customers and non-consumers)

Portfolio Diagnostic

- Identify current/potential innovations (e.g., acquisition targets)

- Evaluate current/planned deployment of innovations; identify opportunities to shape

Identification of selected opportunity and target consumer

Competitor Diagnostic

- Evaluate existing and potential competitors to identify strengths, weaknesses, and blind spots

135

Customer Diagnostic

This diagnostic assesses customers in order to identify "disruptable" market segments. Conducting this diagnostic involves looking for signs that specific customer groups either are overserved or are unsatisfied non-consumers.

Overserved customers consume a product or service but don't need all its features or functionality. Three specific indicators point to this customer group:

1. People complaining about overly complex, expensive products and services.

2. Features that are not valued and therefore are not used.

3. Decreasing price premiums for innovations that historically created value. An overserved customer will say, "Sure, I will take the next version of your product, I just won't pay anything extra for it." For example, according to a January 2, 2004, article in the *Wall Street Journal,* large corporations are increasingly unwilling to pay for expensive upgrades to software programs. This indicates that software providers are overserving increasing swaths of the market.

Where should you look for overserved consumers? The most obvious place is your own customer base. If you find them there, you should immediately curtail investment in improvements in overserved dimensions because customers will not value them. More critically, you need to consider disrupting yourself because there is now room for a competitor to launch a disruptive attack.

The next place to look for overserved customers is in adjacent markets where competitors might be creating an opening for a disruptive assault by overserving their customers.

How should companies determine whether customers are indeed overserved? Interview them. Analyze margins and pricing trends. Read product reviews in industry journals. Quick-and-dirty market research can also help identify the dimensions along which customers are overserved.

The other group of customers to look for is nonconsumers, who generally fall into one of these categories:

1. Consumers who lack specialized skills or training, forcing them to turn to experts to solve important problems.

2. Consumers who lack adequate wealth to participate in a market.

3. Consumers who can use a product or service only in centralized and/or inconvenient settings.

Because nonconsumers lack the ability, wealth, or access to conveniently and easily accomplish an important job for themselves, they typically have to hire someone else to do the job for them or they have to cobble together a less-than-adequate solution.

Nonconsumers exist in every market. Indeed, the first place to look for nonconsumption is in an established market. Mapping a product's or service's delivery chain

> Where should you look for overserved consumers? The most obvious place is your own customer base.

can identify opportunities where removing a link from the delivery chain will allow people to do for themselves what they previously had to rely on others to do for them. The health care industry teems with this kind of nonconsumption. Nonconsumption can also be unearthed by finding out what important jobs customers are seeking to get done that they can't adequately address with current solutions. Closely observing customers and conducting interviews and focus groups can identify these jobs.

One caveat: it's important to understand *why* people

aren't consuming. Sometimes they just don't have a job they are seeking to get done. For example, many people can afford to purchase personal computers but choose not to because there are no jobs that are important enough to them for which the computer would be of assistance.

Portfolio Diagnostic

The portfolio diagnostic assesses whether any current or potential innovations, such as new ideas or acquisition targets that produce appealing innovations, can be deployed in a way that successfully meets the needs of a disruptable customer group. This diagnostic involves looking at the technological characteristics of the innovation and at the potential business model by which the innovation might be brought to market. (See "Portfolio diagnostic.")

A low-end disruptive innovation meets the needs of overserved customers by providing them adequate functionality in return for lower prices. The technology of this sort of disruptive innovation offers "good enough" performance along traditional metrics and is supported by a business model that generates attractive financial returns at low prices. Discount airlines, discount retailers, and index mutual funds all created growth by offering overserved customers "good enough" functionality at lower prices.

Portfolio diagnostic

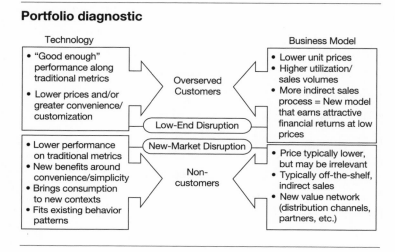

New-market disruptive innovations connect with nonconsumers by making it easier for them to do important jobs themselves. The technology in this category has lower performance along traditional metrics but offers new benefits around convenience, customization, and simplicity that fit squarely with a customer's behavior patterns and priorities. The business model supports these new benefits by typically featuring lower prices and a different, usually simpler, distribution process.

The portfolio diagnostic should identify opportunities to shape innovations, because disruption is almost always a strategic choice. A company can modify a given innovation in ways that enhance its appeal to disruptable customer groups. It can choose the business model that best matches the characteristics of the innovation and the needs of the target customer group.

For example, one electronics company we worked with thought it had a new-market disruptive innovation on its hands. There were two problems with its assessment. First, the innovation offered benefits similar to the company's existing product but at a lower price. Second, the company planned to offer the innovation to its most demanding customers—customers who still were dissatisfied with the performance of the existing product they were purchasing.

This was a mismatch between the innovation and its deployment, but it did not mean the innovation should be scrapped. By performing a customer diagnostic, the company identified overserved customers in an adjacent market who were looking for "good enough" performance at lower prices. The company shaped the innovation into a low-end disruptive innovation targeted at these customers. This strategy provided a better match among the innovation, the target market, and the organization's abilities.

Competitor Diagnostic

The third diagnostic assesses competitors to ensure that the selected opportunity takes unique advantage of their weaknesses and blind spots. First, it helps to evaluate whether a competitor will be motivated to respond. Second, it identifies whether that competitor has the ability to do so effectively.

As coauthors Clayton M. Christensen and Michael E. Raynor discuss in *The Innovator's Solution: Creating and Sustaining Successful Growth,* disruptive innovations typically take advantage of "asymmetries of motivation" by entering markets that incumbents are motivated to exit or ignore. Looking at a competitor's income statement, balance sheet, history of investment decisions, and customers can help identify the developments to which a company might not respond.

Companies tend not to go after opportunities in markets that are too small to meet their growth needs, for instance. They are often happy to shed their least-profitable customers in search of higher-margin opportunities up-market.

> Asymmetric motivation allows a would-be disruptor to hone asymmetric skills.

Companies that introduce disruptive innovations also tend to create asymmetric skills. In other words, they develop the unique ability to do what their competitors are unable to do.

How can you tell what a competitor might not be able

to do? By evaluating its processes—the patterns of inter-action, coordination, communication, and decision making employees use to transform resources into products and services of greater worth. A company's processes determine its skills and strengths as well as its limitations and weaknesses. Why? Processes designed to do one thing often get in the way when companies use them to do something they were not designed to do.

For example, a product development process designed to create complicated high-end products will not be good at creating simple low-end products. Similarly, a distribution process that involves close interaction with sophisticated customers will not be good at working with mass-market retailing channels.

The key then is to identify what processes a competitor has and what processes the company lacks. Processes are developed when companies solve the same problem over and over again. Airplane manufacturers Boeing and Airbus have to coordinate complicated networks of suppliers. Johnson & Johnson has to gain approval for new medical devices. Procter & Gamble has to develop effective product marketing plans. For these companies to be successful, they must have developed ways to repeatedly solve these problems. They need processes to facilitate this.

Determining the tough problems a company has solved to be successful can give insight into its processes, its resultant skills, and its potential weaknesses. The selected opportunity should then require building processes that potential competitors lack.

There is an important connection between asymmetric skills and asymmetric motivation. Asymmetric motivation gives a would-be disruptor time to hone asymmetric skills. How? Even though a competitor could develop the requisite skills to compete successfully during the early days of a disruptive market, it chooses not to. As the would-be disruptor grows, it sharpens its ability to do what the competitor cannot do. This hamstrings future competitive response because the disruptor has the advantage of accumulated learning and knowledge. In other words, asymmetric motivation acts as a shield companies can use to build asymmetric skills.

For example, one chemical company we worked with realized that finding a way to reach nonconsumers in developing countries was its ticket to disruptive growth. It had an in-process innovation that would allow it to dramatically lower the cost of the chemical it produced. Asymmetries of motivation would be on its side if it used the innovation to reach nonconsumers in developing countries; its competitors were not interested in pursuing what seemed to them to be a fringe opportunity. In addition, the chemical company would have to build unique skills to reach the new market, meaning it could race up the experience curve and lock in a sustainable advantage vis-à-vis its competitors. That approach could be the underpinning of a big new-growth business.

Putting It All Together

By systematically conducting these diagnostics, any individual or team can quickly identify which opportunities within its purview are the most promising and therefore merit disproportionate attention. (See "Summary of pattern to seek.") Sometimes, the one or two opportunities worth tackling are exceedingly clear. But other times, a number of seemingly equally promising ideas emerge. In these situations, create a weighting

---

Summary of pattern to seek

Select a high-potential innovation (or several high-potential innovations) that ...

Customers	... connects with an important, unsatisfied job of nonconsumers or gives overserved customers the basics at low prices
Technology	... provides benefits along with new attributes compared with existing technologies
Business Model	... profitably exploits the technology in ways that fit with customer behavior and don't fit with competitors' behavior
Competitors	... takes advantage of asymmetries vis-á-vis existing and potential competitors

---

145

system where each opportunity can be rated against the factors discussed in this article.

When the highest-potential opportunity has been identified, build a preliminary business case for it. It should include a target customer, the characteristics of the selected innovation, the proposed business model to commercialize the innovation, and the predicted competitor response. In addition, the business case should highlight the key unknowns that need to be addressed while the selected opportunity is honed.

These diagnostics can also aid companies that are frustrated by their track record in making acquisitions. Many companies find that large acquisitions provide stable but lackluster returns, whereas small acquisitions typically have highly variable outcomes, occasionally producing blockbuster returns. Screening for small targets that match identified disruptive opportunities can, in essence, cut the tail off the returns distribution curve, allowing companies to capture disruptive growth before it becomes fully understood by the marketplace.

As an added bonus, this analysis will also highlight opportunities for sustaining innovations, the lifeblood of most companies as they allow existing companies to grow within markets where they have already gained a foothold. What kills companies is trying to introduce sustaining innovations into disruptive markets and vice versa.

Rigorously using these three diagnostics can help

avoid this pitfall, allowing companies to systematically identify high-potential opportunities, address gaps between the planned deployment of the innovation and the factors that will determine its success, and begin to create new-growth businesses.

Reprint S0403B

Sometimes a Great Notion Isn't Yet a Great Product

• • •

Clare Martens

Determining whether a new product idea is the right one to take to market can be an expensive and lengthy undertaking. In the journey from concept testing through prototyping to product trials, you must elicit feedback from within your organization; from your partners in design, research, and elsewhere; and, most importantly, from your existing or prospective customers—or both. Whose input you seek, whom you listen to, and whom you ignore will make or break your new product.

But now more than ever, firms are under pressure to come up with new products more quickly even as the budgets available to test such ideas shrink. And so the temptation to cut back is great. "Toward the end of the year, a lot of our clients' budgets are cut," says Jack Gordon, CEO of AcuPOLL Precision Research. "They don't think that in going without $100,000 of testing they'll risk $12 million in introductory money."

The consensus among experts is clear: if you don't do idea testing right, you're likely to regret it later. But that doesn't mean there isn't a great deal of room for improvement over the traditional testing models.

As you consider how you will test your latest idea, it's well worth asking yourself two very basic questions, says Jane Fulton Suri, who leads the human factors discipline at IDEO out of the design firm's San Francisco office. Why are you testing and what do you hope to get out of the experience? As basic as these questions sound, many firms neglect to consider them. Instead they plow forward with established test methods built to do little more than confirm their hunches. Fulton Suri's questions suggest that firms ought to think of idea testing in a much broader fashion: as a way to learn valuable information about both your potential product and your likely customers.

To derive the greatest value from your firm's idea-testing processes, consider these best practices:

1. Judge when to test concept vs. product.

Testing too early or too late in the development cycle can result in wildly misleading results. And so it's vital for firms to determine at what point or points in the innovation process customers can have meaningful experiences with a product idea. At the earliest stages, Fulton Suri suggests drawing a few rough sketches of the product idea being used in context and then talking those concepts through with stakeholders. "Sketching drawings allows people to project onto them and fill them in for themselves," she says. "It's more interactive and provides great open-ended feedback."

But early concept testing doesn't always yield useful results—it depends on the product type. Take Crystal Pepsi. All the concept testing in the early 1990s suggested the proposed colorless drink, positioned to occupy space between cola and lemon-lime soda, would be a hit, says AcuPOLL's Gordon. And so Pepsi moved ahead with bringing the product to market. And it bombed. Why? Consumers as a whole didn't have a positive experience with the product, which didn't have a distinctive flavor of its own. Emboldened by its strong early concept testing, Pepsi apparently didn't test the product with nearly enough vigor. As a result, the company wasted untold millions developing and marketing what should have never escaped R&D.

2. Test early and often.

Once you start prototyping, test early and often and don't hesitate to demonstrate unfinished models. In 1998, IDEO worked with Kodak on the interface architecture for one of the company's first consumer digital cameras, the DC210. In search of feedback on a product category that was still a very new concept for many consumers, IDEO built a prototype three times larger than the hand-held device's actual size. The larger model allowed consumers to more easily appreciate its features and to really put the various camera buttons and their functions through their paces. Drawing an analogy to regular cameras, many consumers wondered aloud where the film was and how much film was left, useful feedback on how important it was for the camera to indicate how much memory remained.

"The more you can prototype and show the prototype the better," says Ken Tameling, group leader for seating at office furniture company Steelcase. The company had upward of 16 prototypes for its Leap office chair. Steelcase's close observation of test subjects as they sat and reclined in early prototypes of the chair led the firm and its partners to develop two technologies that greatly enhanced the product, says Tameling: Live Back technology, which allows the chair's back to "morph to the way the spine wants to move," and the Natural Glide System technology, which causes the seat to glide forward as the user reclines.

3. Seek testers who can add unique value.

From feedback on the first Leap prototype to include Live Back technology, Steelcase learned that users would need separate upper and lower back controls. To help make the controls more intuitive, they tested the product with the Michigan Council of the Blind. The Council's feedback suggested having all paddle controls for the seat and all knob controls for the back, which Steelcase hadn't previously considered.

4. Listen for the unexpected.

The German consumer goods firm Beiersdorf had an idea for a body lotion featuring light-reflecting pigment that would make skin imperfections less noticeable. "When we first put the idea out there, we didn't talk about moisturizing," says Jim Dunne, the marketing research manager for Beiersdorf. But as the firm listened to feedback during concept testing, they learned that for the product's target customers, moisturizing was important. So developers refocused marketing efforts to promote the product's moisturizing properties.

When Nivea Body Silky Shimmer Lotion hit the stores in 2002, Dunne says, "it was one of our big successes. It was an idea that people had been looking out for."

Savvy product testers listen to feedback with an ear toward the unexpected and the ambiguous. And, they won't hesitate to probe for clarity's sake. Consider this consumer comment, IDEO's Fulton Suri says: "I need two hands to do this." The comment could be taken to mean the product needs two handles or that the single handle wasn't designed well enough for one-handed use.

5. Maintain a safe emotional distance.

"Some people become so enthusiastic and wedded to their own idea that they become deaf to feedback that it might be bad," says David Reibstein, professor of marketing at the University of Pennsylvania's Wharton School.

He highlights the example of the Jiminy Cricket Wishing Stars breakfast cereal created by Post Cereals in 1982 and championed by a company executive against all the odds. The cereal was based around the character Jiminy Cricket, best known for his song "When You Wish Upon a Star" in the 1940 animated film *Pinocchio*. Children in the early 1980s had no idea who Jiminy Cricket was and "all the test results on the cereal came back negative," says Reibstein. "The executive couldn't care less because he believed in it." Needless to say, once launched, Wishing Stars was a failure.

In idea testing, companies "must be willing to have their ideas disconfirmed," says Robert Sutton, professor of management science and engineering at Stanford University and author of *Weird Ideas That Work*.

6. Test the context, too.

You've got a great idea, but are you fully probing how your product will fit in the context of the existing market? When you're market testing, you need to ask, "Is there a prevailing paradigm that might be relatively difficult to shift?" says Fulton Suri. She recalls working on an innovative two-handed game control that had fantastic performance. But to the surprise of IDEO and its client, the device didn't do well in the market. The joystick was the prevailing paradigm for playing video games, and there was simply no appetite in the market to try something new. The testing process didn't measure the product's likelihood for use in the current market conditions; it tested only for feedback on actual product performance.

7. Seek naive users.

When testing out prototypes, Sutton suggests involving people who are totally unfamiliar with that product. "Nonexperts who've never used something are better at figuring out how to use it and estimating the time it takes to use it," he says. Sutton cites research by Pamela

Hinds, assistant professor in management science and engineering at Stanford University, who found that people with moderate or zero knowledge of using cell phones are better than the phones' designers at estimating how long it takes to learn a task on the phones.

8. If all else fails, go with your gut.

In the end, should your testing yield contradictory or ambiguous results, trust in what you think is right based on all the information. "I was on a panel with [venture capitalist] Brook Byers from Kleiner Perkins Caufield & Byers," Sutton recalls, "and he talked about sustaining advantage by trimming away the weeds and watering the flowers. I said, 'How do you know which are the weeds and which are the flowers?' He said, 'Sometimes you have to guess. You can't water everything. You have to focus on doing just a few things well, and ignore everything else.'"

Reprint U0403C

Is Your Product-Development Process Helping— or Hindering— Innovation?

• • •

Eric Mankin

In the fall of 2004, Danger introduced its hiptop2 device, a super cell phone. Selling for $300, the all-in-one communication device has a color screen and camera, and can serve as a phone, Internet browser, e-mail device, personal organizer, and instant-messaging apparatus.

Service providers were excited by the product. Danger is a privately held company and does not disclose sales figures, but eight wireless carriers in six countries currently offer the hiptop2. In the United States, the product is being sold nationwide by T-Mobile.

The developmental evolution of Danger's original hiptop device (the hiptop2 is the newest generation of the original product) didn't follow accepted best practices for corporate product development, which call for a stage-gate or phase-gate approach to the process. Under this framework, projects move in a linear fashion from one phase of the development process to the next after passing through a gate review by senior management. The gate reviews allow managers to filter out those projects that appear to be less attractive to the company and emphasize projects that seem to have greater profit potential.

Rather, the device came about through a more circular, more flexible, iterative product design process that allowed designers to repeatedly garner—then react to—feedback about their product while they were developing it.

When companies use stage-gate processes exclusively, they run the risk of missing big opportunities in emerging markets or new technologies. Indeed, when constructed around a stage-gate template, such opportunities typically run into difficulty as early as the second stage of the process, when the development team tries to build a business case for their product. It's hard to construct a compelling justification for a product or process when the market—and even the product itself—remains undefined, as was the case with Danger's hiptop device.

Evolution of a "Peanut"

Joe Britt, Danger's cofounder and chief technology officer, described the device's developmental progression in a recent interview. "We worked on our original product—which we called the 'peanut'—during the first six months of 2000. It was designed to be a nano-PDA—a tiny, cheap personal digital assistant that could fit on a key chain. It connected to a computer via a small dock and was very different from the hiptop product we launched in 2002."

Danger took its peanut to investors, who asked the designers to make it wireless. Once the peanut was wireless, the same investors suggested it should also have two-way communication, enabling it to send information to the computer as well as receive information from it. Adding this two-way communication helped Danger's founders to envision further expansions of their product's capabilities. Clearly, Danger's current hiptop product would likely not have been created had the designers not cycled through the iterative process.

Though the stage-gate approach has improved product-development processes—by making projects visible to the organization as they progress through the stages and gates to launch, by offering a structured way for senior management to be involved, and by providing a disciplined way for senior managers to give direction—it's most effective with projects targeted at specific, well-defined markets. Originally conceived by Professor Robert Cooper of the University of Western Ontario, the process, as illustrated by Cooper's Product Development Institute, looks like "The stage-gate product development process."

Since Cooper first detailed this approach in his 1986 book, *Winning at New Products: Accelerating the Process from Idea to Launch,* the stage-gate process has become the sole method most large companies use to bring new products to market, primarily because it offers an increase in development productivity, faster time to market, and a reduction in schedule slip rates.

Tailor the Process to the Project

Companies faced with new, evolving markets or technologies, however, would be better served by using the more fluid iterative approach, which looks like "An iterative product-development process."

The success of many new products depends on developers conducting a dialogue with their target market—offering a product, monitoring its acceptance, then adjusting it to attract more customers. This is the

The stage-gate product development process

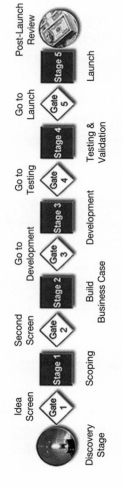

| Discovery Stage | Gate 1 Idea Screen | Stage 1 Scoping | Gate 2 Second Screen | Stage 2 Build Business Case | Gate 3 Go to Development | Stage 3 Development | Gate 4 Go to Testing | Stage 4 Testing & Validation | Gate 5 Go to Launch | Stage 5 Launch | Post-Launch Review |

An iterative product-development process

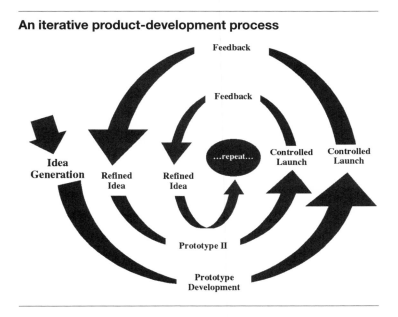

essence of the iterative approach. This takes time, however, and requires a substantial degree of customer and company education—not to mention flexibility on the part of the company and its development team—and a willingness to listen and respond to what the market has to say.

The iterative approach is far more effective at delivering a marketable, successful solution when markets are new or evolving, and customer needs are emerging and have not yet been clearly expressed, because the existence of the product influences customers' need for the product. In emerging markets, customers often don't know they need a product until they have a chance to see one and try it. And when they see their feedback acted upon and incorporated into the product, this only serves to enhance their desire for it.

There's an additional payoff to using the iterative approach. Market feedback can help pinpoint precisely where the next round of adjustments should be made.

Iterations can point to a change in usage.

Consider the experience of Jeff Hawkins and Donna Dubinsky, the creators of the original Palm electronic organizer. Perhaps the most important insight in the Palm's development came after one of its predecessors, the Zoomer, failed in the marketplace. Pursuing an interactive development approach, the Palm executives commissioned market research to understand how the few customers who had purchased the Zoomer actually used it. Research revealed that those who had bought the product were looking for a complement to their personal computers. Thus was born synchronization and the format that continues to dominate the PDA market.

Iterations can lead to a change in form.

When Sharp launched its Wizard Organizer in 1988, the product's keyboard was arranged alphabetically, with the letter A at the upper left and Z at the bottom right. Customers quickly made it clear they preferred a

QWERTY keypad, so Sharp's next, more successful, version of the product used that layout.

Iterations can help a company develop and build the market for a product.

Prior to the mid-1990s, the antidepressant market in Japan was minuscule. The country's culture viewed depression as a stigmatizing disability that could be treated only in a hospital or sanatorium.

Eli Lilly, which invented Prozac (the drug that pioneered the category of antidepressant medications was launched in the United States in 1988), used a stage-gate approach when it studied the feasibility of introducing Prozac to Japan shortly after the U.S. introduction. Lilly decided not to enter the Japanese market because there was no expressed customer need. Any company running a stage-gate process would have come to a similar conclusion.

Still, there were compelling indications that the need was there, although unrecognized and undeveloped. The suicide rate in Japan, for example, is about double the rate in the United States, signaling that depression might be a problem. But the development of the market for antidepressant medication in Japan required repeated rounds of education of both patients and doctors. Each iteration was built on the previous effort.

First came the commitment by a company to bring an antidepressant to the market. Ichiro Kitasato, the president of Tokyo-based pharmaceuticals firm Meiji Seika Kaisha, viewed it as an opportunity to link up with the Belgian pharmaceuticals and chemicals giant Solvay and, along with partner Fujisawa Pharmaceuticals, to market the antidepressant Luvox in the late 1980s. "People in the company said there are too few patients in Japan," he told the *Wall Street Journal*. "But I looked at the U.S. and Europe . . . and thought [Japan] is sure to be a big market."

After commitment came a stroke of luck that helped initiate consumer education. In 1996, one of the major Japanese television networks aired a prime-time documentary on antidepressant medications. After the show, 2,000 viewers called to thank the network for publicizing the situation.

The education of Japanese patients continued with market development activities that repositioned depression as a relatively common, treatable disease. In 1999, Meiji Seika and its partners created an advertising campaign in Japan introducing the possibility that a person's soul can have a cold—*kokoro no kaze* in Japanese. The idea behind the phrase is simple: if you take medicine for a cold, you should be able to take something when you're depressed as well.

Market development then moved from advertising to the Internet, where potential customers could find articles on depression and the benefits that pharmaceuticals provide. Efforts in market education were amplified and reinforced by increasing press coverage and public discussion of depression.

As a result, during the past 10 years, there has been a radical change in perspective on the part of the Japanese population. And with this shift, the market for antidepressant medication in Japan has grown rapidly. Glaxo-SmithKline, for example, launched Paxil in Japan in December 2000. Sales reached $96.5 million in 2001. Sales of Luvox and Depromel—the name under which Luvox is sold by Meiji's marketing partner, Fujisawa—totaled about $116.5 million in 2002. In 2003, Glaxo reported 27% growth in Paxil's international sales, driven by strong growth in Japan.

Meanwhile, Lilly, the global market leader in antidepressant medication, was only able to launch Prozac in Japan in 2004 and still lags behind its competitors in that market. The company's decision to stay away from the Japanese market in the early 1990s made sense within the context of its stage-gate process but has proved to be a costly decision.

Stay Open to Possibilities

In some situations, companies focused on serving an existing or emerging market might discover that they lack the best technology to address their product development needs. Increasingly, solutions to technical problems are readily available for purchase, usually at a cost that is much lower than the cost of internal development. Professor Henry Chesbrough at the University of California, Berkeley's Haas School of Business reports that companies that follow a carefully planned idea-solicitation process—often via the Internet—can expect to receive an average of 10 high-quality proposals and, in some cases, will get as many as 40.

Unfortunately, most companies don't know when or how to look outside their own boundaries to find these solutions; in addition, they often don't know exactly what they're looking for. The stage-gate process, with its emphasis on rapid movement from one gate to another, is not designed to encourage external search. On the other hand, because the iterative approach orients a project toward market exploration, it will frequently lead to searching for existing technical solutions as well. For example, as Danger was trying to make its peanut wireless, it came to rely on a radio technology called DARC, or Data Audio Radio Channel, which came from a Japanese company. The technology is used to broadcast information that the device receives.

Searching for existing technical solutions continues to get easier. There are now several new companies, such as NineSigma and InnoCentive, that aim to match technological problems and solutions. InnoCentive, for example, pairs up scientists in chemistry and biology with companies looking for specific solutions.

Fit Your Process to Your Product, Not the Other Way Around

In 1962, the eminent historian Alfred D. Chandler Jr. published *Strategy and Structure: Chapters in the History of the American Industrial Enterprise,* a historical review of the interrelationship between a business's strategy and its organization. He recommended a clear hierarchical relationship between the two: structure as a servant to strategy. All too often, Chandler's research found that a business's structure served as an impediment to the success of its strategy, with profoundly negative consequences.

Today, due largely to blind acceptance of industry practices, the product-development processes of many companies also serve as an impediment, rather than an enabler, to the success of many new products. To be successful, companies need to fit their product-development processes to the needs of their product concepts, rather than the reverse.

Reprint S0411C

Disruption Is a Moving Target

• • •

Scott D. Anthony

There's an old adage that poignantly illustrates one of the fundamental challenges would-be innovators face: "It is easy to identify the pioneers. They're the ones with the arrows in their backs." All too frequently, the company or person that forges the way and establishes a market gets attacked and toppled by competitors not willing to take the risks related to being a pioneer.

In the business arena, this plays out again and again. A decade ago, Netscape created the browser market before getting crushed by Microsoft. Tom Siebel left Oracle in 1993 to found his eponymous company, Siebel Systems, selling customer relationship management

(CRM) software that improves a business's abilities to manage sales programs. Software giant SAP initially missed the CRM market, entered late, but was projected to overtake Siebel Systems and become the leader in this category. Indeed, Siebel had already begun to feel the arrow's sting: its stock dropped by 94% between 2000 and 2003.

Many wonder if the same fate will befall TiVo, whose innovative digital video recorder (DVR) has made believers of millions of users but faces challenges as it seeks to continue to grow.

How can you tell when a white-hot upstart might end up with arrows in its back? Entrants that follow a disruptive path—creating growth by bringing new benefits around simplicity, convenience, customization, and low prices—can often avoid the arrows and blaze new trails. But sometimes companies that seem to be following a disruptive strategy don't end up toppling incumbents and reshaping industries.

When Disruptive Beginnings Don't Lead to Disruptive Ends

When companies use asymmetries to their advantage, they can introduce disruptive innovations that create growth and reshape industries. The typical pattern starts with an incumbent ignoring an initial entrant's growth and continues with an entrant's incursions into an incumbent's businesses, leading to an incumbent's flight, rather than fight. Ultimately, it ends with the entrant overtaking the incumbent. But when something doesn't fit the pattern—when an entrant is interested in the initial market, when industry economics motivate an incumbent to fight rather than flee, or when an entrant makes choices that dull its disruptive edge—companies that seem poised for success can suddenly derail.

Incumbents consider the innovation to be sustaining.

Because potential disruptors are usually small and nimble, they often can spot opportunities before larger incumbents. However, entrants need to be careful not to assume that initial disinterest automatically means an incumbent is disruptable. If an entrant introduces an innovation that looks sustaining through the eyes of well-resourced competitors, once the entrant proves a market exists, the incumbent can marshal its resources to fight back.

Both Siebel and TiVo illustrate this situation. Siebel moved more quickly than SAP to create the CRM software industry. However, from SAP's perspective, CRM looked like an innovation that sustained the performance of SAP's enterprise resource planning software, which helps manage things such as a company's manufacturing and procurement processes. SAP's most important customers wanted the ability to improve their sales efforts, too. CRM slotted nicely into SAP's market-leading software, and SAP's ability to knit CRM processes with other processes included in its software allowed it to produce a better product than Siebel could.

Similarly, TiVo came up with an unquestionably innovative idea, producing a piece of hardware that allows people to record shows digitally and watch them whenever they want. In fact, it created an entire market. However, DVR technology looks highly sustaining to a number of industry players.

Once cable companies knew that customers wanted to be able to watch what they wanted, when they wanted, they began to experiment with ways to offer competing services. They asked set-top-box manufacturers such as Motorola and Scientific-Atlanta to include DVR functionality in their cable boxes. Because set-top-box manufacturers and cable companies control the interface with the customer, they can knit together solutions that specialist players such as TiVo just can't.

So instead of having the market to itself, TiVo is forced to fend off counterattacks by motivated, well-financed players wishing to capture the value that TiVo has created. TiVo is now responding by building new revenue streams. Although this might be successful, TiVo is spending a lot of money racing away from the market it created.

Industry structure makes fight, not flight, natural.

When incumbents don't find flight attractive, disruption is exceedingly difficult. If incumbents lack the ability to

How Asymmetries Power Disruption

Understanding precisely how disruption works can help you pinpoint which initiatives are truly disruptive and which merely look that way. The keys to disruption are asymmetries—when one company does something its opponent either doesn't want to do or doesn't have the ability to do. Disruption typically follows a three-step process:

1. **Disruptors enter a market incumbents don't care about.** Disruptors either target the low end of an established market, reaching customers overshot by existing offerings (think discount retailers), or they create new markets by competing against nonconsumption (think personal computers). Typically, incumbents lack the impetus to go after or defend the very market entrants are motivated to serve. Either the customers within that market are an incumbent's least profitable or the market seems too inconsequential. So the incumbent ignores the disruptive developments or exits the markets the entrant is targeting. This asymmetric motivation acts as a shield that protects a disruptor in its early days.

2. **Entrants grow as incumbents flee.** As entrants improve their products or services, they begin to make inroads into progressively more demanding market tiers. When the incumbent feels the threat, its natural motivation is to flee rather than fight.

   Conflict first becomes apparent among an incumbent's least demanding customers since they are attracted by the disruptor's low prices or relatively straightforward (generally not high-performance) offerings. At this point, incumbents typically face a choice: invest to defend their least profitable business or invest to produce better products that allow them to charge higher prices to more demanding customers in the high end of their market. The natural inclination is to leave the lower-end business in search of more profitable opportunities up market. Again, the disruptive attacker has asymmetric motivation, since, at this point, even the least-performance-demanding customers in an established market look very attractive.

3. **The incumbent hits a ceiling.** The flight to the high end described above cannot continue forever. As more and more customers at higher tiers of the market jump ship, it grows increasingly clear that incumbents need to fight back. However, by the time they realize this, it's typically too late. The entrant that has hidden behind the shield of asymmetric motivation has had time to develop the unique skills needed to deliver new benefits related to simplicity, customization, and low prices. And it has forged relationships with a new set of partners to support its disruptive business model.

   Incumbent skills that are strengths in their core market don't help them respond effectively to disruption. As the game shifts to the one the disruptor plays, it becomes very difficult for the incumbent to respond at all because the entrant is doing precisely what the incumbent can't do.

move up market or aren't motivated to leave the low end, they opt to fight as soon as they sense a threat. These struggles result in bruising battles for market share, where the victor's prize is a spoiled business.

The clearest example of this circumstance is the airline industry, where discount airlines such as JetBlue Airways and ATA Airlines have entered the low end of the industry but have encountered stiff response by leading incumbents such as American Airlines and Delta Air Lines, which have neither the ability to move up market nor the motivation to leave the low end.

Would leading airlines like to offer premium services that allow them to reach higher market tiers? Of course. There are many dimensions along which customers would be quite willing to pay premium prices, such as shorter flights or guarantees of on-time arrival. However, airlines just don't have the ability to guarantee those dimensions in order to move up market.

Are leading airlines motivated to shed less-demanding customers who are looking for the lowest possible prices? Hardly. Running an airline is an extremely complicated, risky endeavor, involving high fixed costs. Leading providers operate fleets of aircraft that cost hundreds of millions of dollars. They have tens of thousands of employees overseeing their far-flung route structure. Despite these high costs, the incremental cost of flying an additional passenger is low. Therefore, airlines are motivated to spread their fixed costs over as many passengers as possible. They would much rather have a customer pay a low price than fly a plane with even a single empty seat.

So, although discounters have a cost structure that allows them to make money at lower price points, when they begin taking customers away from established firms, the established firms have no choice but to fight back. The fact that airlines can dynamically adjust the

> Disruption is a strategic choice. Companies can follow a disruptive strategy or morph in ways that allow incumbents to benefit.

price of an individual seat provides them with an effective response tactic. When JetBlue started flying routes from Boston to Oakland, CA, and Orlando, FL, American immediately responded by slashing prices on those routes and offering customers who flew two trips on similar routes free tickets anywhere American flew. When JetBlue tried to break into Delta's hub in Atlanta, Delta slashed prices and added 50% more flights, driving JetBlue from the market.

People often point to Southwest Airlines' 33 years of success as a counterexample to this point. However, most of its success has not come from a head-on fight against incumbents. Instead, it has largely chosen to fly point-to-point routes between second-tier airports in cities such as Providence and Baltimore. Because it has not directly attacked incumbents, it has been able to grow for 33 years without incurring response.

Generally, incumbents are motivated to fight rather than flee when sizable up-front expenditures need to be amortized over a large number of users and the marginal cost of serving an additional customer is low.

Entrants make choices that lower the disruptive nature of their business models.

Disruption is typically a strategic choice. Companies can choose to follow a disruptive strategy or lower the chances they will disrupt incumbents by morphing their strategy in ways that make it easier for incumbents to benefit.

For example, regional airlines, which fly out of airports in small, out-of-the-way cities that traditional airlines are not motivated to serve, brim with disruptive energy. They have a lower-cost business model than traditional airlines. However, regional airlines have almost universally chosen to complement rather than disrupt leading providers. Specifically, they've followed a strategy of feeding customers onto existing hub-and-spoke networks instead of creating complementary networks.

In 2002, more than 60% of regional airlines' flights fed on to the hub-and-spoke infrastructure of the large airlines. To fit into the existing network, regional airlines had to integrate their business tightly with the large airlines by sharing gates and using code-share agreements to allow a customer to buy a ticket from multiple operators at once. Instead of looking like potential threats to incumbents, they ended up looking like partners.

Generally, companies that place themselves in an established value network—a community comprising an incumbent and the incumbent's suppliers, channels, and partners—have to adapt their strategy to conform to the value network's common goals and operating models. This conformity lessens their disruptive potential and increases the chances that incumbents will see value in "co-opting" the new strategy.

As regional airlines grew, existing operators were highly motivated to capture a piece of that growth. Delta purchased Comair in late 1999. It also owns Atlantic Southeast Airlines. American owns American Eagle, which owns Executive Airlines, Flagship Airlines, Simmons Airlines, and Wings West Airlines. Before its initial public offering in 2002, ExpressJet Holdings (which flies under the name of Continental Express) was a wholly owned subsidiary of Continental. Continental retains a 53% ownership stake. By choosing a complementary strategy, regional airlines may have increased their chance of survival, but they have lowered their chances of disrupting existing providers.

This line of thinking can help suggest what JetBlue

should do to maximize the chances that it continues to create disruptive growth. It should seek to compete against nonconsumption, flying routes that existing players find unprofitable. It should seek to minimize points of interaction with incumbent value networks. Fortunately for JetBlue's investors, it seems to be headed in that direction. In 2003, JetBlue announced plans to purchase a large number of regional jets. If it uses these jets to cobble together a de facto national network that doesn't interact with leading airlines' hub-and-spoke networks, it could develop a strategy that has a much higher chance of success.

Happy Disruptive Ending?

Not all stories that start with a chapter on disruption end happily. Look at the particular circumstances to identify if a company that seems to have started down the road to disruptive wealth is likely to succeed or to get ambushed along the way. Ask if the innovation appears sustaining to any well-resourced competitors. Check to see if industry circumstances allow incumbents to flee, instead of fight, when threatened. And carefully watch the choices entrants make as they shape and develop their strategy to ensure they are embracing, not erasing, their disruptive edge.

Reprint S0407D

Are You Reading the Right Signals?

• • •

Clayton M. Christensen and Scott D. Anthony

All of us make countless decisions every day based on what we think the future will hold. Some decisions are more fraught with risk than others. Investors purchase stock in companies that seem poised to take off; analysts generate reports predicting industry trends; consultants issue make-or-break recommendations to their clients.

The challenge, naturally, is that the future rarely turns out as expected. Promising companies suddenly fizzle out; an analyst's predictions turn out to be 100% wrong; consultants unintentionally point their clients in the wrong directions. Predicting the future is a frustrating endeavor. This is especially true for volatile industries, such as the U.S. telecommunications industry.

Consider the pattern that innovation in the telecom-munications industry has followed over the past decade. Deregulation in 1996 created a huge wave of excitement and hype, but most of the companies and technologies introduced in the late 1990s drove little real change. Then, just as hype dissipated, technologies and compa-nies capable of driving real industry change quietly began to appear.

This pattern demonstrates one of the most pressing challenges facing people trying to predict future trends: determining whether a hyped innovation truly has the potential to transform an industry. Take, for example, three industry developments in recent years:

1. The emergence of Skype Technologies, a provider of free Internet-based telephony services by the duo that created Kazaa (the file-swapping software that allows people to share music over the Internet).

2. Industry legend Craig McCaw's announcement in June that his latest venture, Clearwire, would offer high-speed "fixed wireless" broadband solutions.

3. Little-discussed efforts by America Online and other instant messaging (IM) providers to make it easier for people to use the simple technology to hold audio conferences and videoconferences.

Which of these developments are transformational, and which will end up being more hype than reality? In this article, we discuss how the analytical approach laid out in our recent book, *Seeing What's Next: Using the Theories of Innovation to Predict Industry Change,* coauthored with Erik A. Roth, can help answer that question. The fact that each of these developments either occurred or came into sharper focus after the book was written demonstrates the industry's dynamic nature.

Our analysis suggests that these developments provide further evidence that the telecommunications industry is on the brink of substantial transformation. Critical yet-to-be-made choices will still determine who ends up on top when the dust settles, but it is clear the future will be substantially different from the present.

Skype: VoIP from the Fringe

One of the most often discussed technologies in telecommunications is VoIP (Voice over Internet Protocol), which involves using the Internet to transmit voice calls over a data network. The quality of a VoIP call is slightly lower than that of a traditional phone call. VoIP offerings lack other key features such as "line powering," which allows a traditional phone to work even if the electrical power goes out. VoIP uses networks extremely efficiently, however, allowing providers to charge lower prices per call. And the technology is both flexible and customizable.

We believe that although the emergence of new VoIP

providers such as Vonage seems to signal impending low-end disruption, incumbents are likely to "co-opt" that technology and offer it to their core customers.

Why? VoIP providers are targeting the core business of the leading local telephony incumbents (in the United States, these include Verizon, SBC Communications, BellSouth, and Qwest). Because telecommunications is a

> Companies seeking to create disruptive growth have a better chance of success if they minimize points of interaction with competitors' value networks.

high fixed-cost business in which providers historically have focused on "universal service," incumbents are motivated to fight for each and every customer. Therefore, it is predictable that every leading North American telecommunications provider has announced a VoIP strategy.

Skype Technologies, founded by Niklas Zennström and Janus Friis, is taking a different approach to VoIP.

The company introduced a trial version of its peer-to-peer software in August 2003. Customers using the program can send and receive calls from their personal computer to other Skype users around the world. The application is free and simple to download and install, and the calls are free and of high quality.

Skype's emergence clearly signals industry change. The company's product is competing against nonconsumption by bringing voice communication into completely new contexts. As of July 2004, more than 17 million copies of its software had been downloaded. In April 2004, Skype introduced a version of its software that allows users to place and receive free Skype calls on mobile devices connected to high-speed Wi-Fi, or Wireless Fidelity, networks.

Skype is taking advantage of powerful asymmetries that might prove to be real assets once competitive battles break out. Skype is focusing on a new market application. Its business model further limits the chance of incumbent response. Instead of charging for phone calls, Skype plans to make money by selling services (such as voicemail) and advertisements. To mimic Skype's model, incumbents would have to give away their core product. Finally, while Skype is hiding behind this shield of asymmetric motivation, the skills it is developing related to software development and managing data applications will further limit the ability of competitors to respond.

One of the critical strategic choices Skype faces is

whether it wants to expand beyond its freestanding value network, which requires both the person making the call and the person receiving the call to use Skype's software. Generally, companies seeking to create disruptive growth have a better chance of success if they minimize points of interaction with competitors' value networks because this allows the entrants to sharpen their disruptive edge while limiting a competitor's ability to keep a close eye on the solution.

One potentially troubling sign is that Skype has attracted investment from top-shelf venture capitalists such as Bessemer Venture Partners and Draper Fisher Jurvetson. Implicit in such investment is the hope that Skype can grow rapidly; yet the need to grow quickly might force Skype to move its business model in a direction similar to that of Vonage and other VoIP providers, which are targeting large, existing markets instead of trying to create new markets.

To do this, Skype might have to leave its freestanding value network and enter into an overlapping network, dulling its disruptive edge. Indeed, in June, Skype quietly introduced a beta version of an application called Skype-Out, which allows users to purchase prepaid minutes to reach people on conventional phones outside of Skype's network.

Skype could continue to evolve and drive industry change, however, if Skype's investors encourage the company to be patient for growth—but impatient for profits—until it finds a viable business model.

Clearwire: A Legend Returns

Clearwire's CEO Craig McCaw has a history of shaking up the telecommunications industry. McCaw Cellular, which he founded in 1981, became the first truly nationwide mobile telephony provider before being acquired by AT&T for $11.5 billion in 1994. McCaw then went on to develop Nextel, whose popular "push-to-talk" service drove that company to a multibillion-dollar market capitalization.

McCaw's track record is not a string of unbroken successes, however. XO Communications, which attempted to crack into the local telephony market, went bankrupt in 2002. Teledesic, which hoped to provide satellite-delivered Internet service, never launched a satellite.

McCaw hopes to add Clearwire to his string of successes. Using a small device they can install themselves, customers will be able to receive high-speed, wireless access to the Internet. The device has to be stationary to work, hence the name "fixed wireless." Clearwire obviates the need to obtain a high-speed connection from the cable or phone company.

Clearwire's business model has several key elements that enhance its ability to reach customers. First, it can charge low prices because its solution does not require building expensive networks. Second, Clearwire owns an equipment company called NextNet Wireless. End-to-end control over the service and the equipment it offers

How to See What's Next

In our book, *Seeing What's Next*, we suggest following a three-part process for using innovation theories to predict industry change.

First, look for *signals of change,* signs of companies emerging to meet the needs of three different customer groups: undershot customers, for whom existing solutions aren't good enough; overshot customers, for whom existing solutions are too good; and nonconsuming customers—those who lack the skills, wealth, or ability to benefit from existing solutions.

Signs of undershot customers include consumers eagerly snatching up new products, steady or increasing prices, and the struggles of companies offering products with basic features. Undershot customers look for sustaining innovations that close the gap between what is available and what they're looking to accomplish.

Overshot customers consider existing solutions to be too good. Indications that overshot customers exist include customer reluctance to purchase new versions of products, declining prices, and the emergence of companies offering products with basic features. Over-

customers should give Clearwire the flexibility to iron out significant bugs and make its solution more usable. For example, the company claims that users will be able to install its device in 15 minutes—without expert assistance.

Clearwire's most important strategic option relates to

shot customers welcome low-end disruptive innovations that offer sufficient technological performance at low prices.

Signs of nonconsumption include customers who have to turn to someone with greater skills or training for service; a market limited to those with great wealth; and the need to go to centralized, inconvenient locations to consume. Nonconsumers welcome new-market disruptive innovations that make it simpler and more convenient for them to solve problems themselves.

Although most analysis of industry change focuses on the most undershot customers (often termed "lead" customers), watching for the innovations that have the most potential to drive industry change actually requires paying careful attention to the least demanding, most overshot customers and nonconsumers seemingly on the fringe of the market.

The second part of the process requires analyzing *competitive battles* to see which firms are likely to emerge triumphant. There are two components to this analysis. The first is *taking the tale of the tape,* to identify each combatant's strengths, weaknesses, and blind spots. Taking

the customer group it chooses to target. There are three paths Clearwire could follow. The first would be to compete against consumption at the high end of the market, trying to bring a premium service to performance-demanding customers. Clearwire does not appear to be following this approach, and that's good. Given the

the tale of the tape involves evaluating a company's resources (what it has), processes (the way it does business), and values (the rules that determine how its resources are allocated). Most of the analysis should focus on processes, which determine what a company can and cannot do, and values, which determine what a company will and will not do. The second component requires looking for the company with asymmetries on its side, the one that is doing what its opponent has neither the skills nor the motivation to do.

The third part of the process evaluates *strategic choices* that can help to determine ultimate winners and losers. When assessing entrants, see whether the company is following a preparation regimen that facilitates it finding a disruptive path. Check the management team's schools of experience, verify that the company is

unpredictable nature of new technologies, Clearwire's first product would likely have limitations that would disappoint these customers.

Clearwire's second option would be to compete against nonconsumption. Clearwire could try to go to areas in lesser-developed countries that lack the infrastructure to receive any kind of broadband service. Although this path would be difficult, it would have real potential to drive disruptive growth.

The final path, and the one Clearwire appears to be following, is a hybrid, low-end/new-market strategy. The low-end portion would target customers that purchase encouraging emergent forces, and confirm that the company's investors will allow it to follow a disruptive path.

Next, check to see how entrants are choosing value network participants such as suppliers, distributors, and ancillary partners. Entrants residing in freestanding value networks that do not interact with incumbents have the greatest chance of driving industry change; entrants located within an established value network create the possibility of incumbent co-option.

Finally, look to see whether incumbents have earned their disruptive black belts by developing the capability to capitalize on disruptive trends. Incumbents that have nurtured this capability could respond to a disruptive threat by setting up a separate organization or using an established process to parry the disruptive attacker.

existing solutions but find them too expensive and too complicated. The new-market portion would seek to increase the market by reaching customers previously locked out of it.

The closer Clearwire adheres to a disruptive path, marketing to nonconsumers or overshot customers, the greater its chances of success. One structural factor that works in its favor is that broadband penetration in the United States is about 20%, which means that incumbents have significant headroom to march up market.

How can you assess whether Clearwire is likely to stick

to the disruptive path? In our book, we suggest looking at a company's preparation regimen: its management team, strategy-making process, and investors.

For Clearwire, signs are promising on all fronts. The company seems to be following an emergent strategy emphasizing experimentation and flexibility. It launched in only two markets this summer and plans to expands to 20 markets in 2005. McCaw himself controls Clearwire, meaning Clearwire's investors will not force the company to grow too quickly. Finally, McCaw's experi-

> Incumbents to bet on are those that recognize that they need to do things differently to capitalize on emerging technologies.

ence has taught him the promise and peril of different approaches. Overall, Clearwire seems to have an excellent chance to drive disruptive growth.

IM: Disruption Continues to Flower

Although VoIP still generates the most hype, an innovation that has potentially as much transformational power quietly chugs along behind it.

Instant messaging first took root as a simple way for teenagers to send short, snappy correspondence to each other. Millions of users have downloaded the free software offered by America Online, Microsoft, and Yahoo.

Today, the number of corporations using IM technology is growing; IBM and Microsoft are offering enterprise-grade products to improve the way they meet the more demanding needs of corporate users.

Notice that none of these players are traditional communications providers. These developments are true signals of change. Instant messaging technology brings communication capabilities into entirely new contexts, and users communicate in completely different ways than they do when using the telephone. Providers are using IM technology to broaden their own business models, which were already different from the business models of most communications providers.

In *Seeing What's Next,* we noted that the critical thing to watch is how IM providers move up market by adding new services. In June, AOL announced deals with WebEx Communications and Lightbridge to provide Web meetings and conference calls over instant messaging technologies.

AOL decided to charge for the service, which ultimately could turn out to be a mistake because that doesn't fit with IM's free and simple value proposition. It shows, however, how IM providers are moving closer to becoming true telecommunications players, further fanning the disruptive flames.

Summary

Overall, the technologies discussed here generally appear to be threats to established market leaders. Entrants that continue to develop distinctive business models that reach nonconsumers or bring consumption to new contexts have a real chance to drive industry change.

Established companies that play their cards right and view these technologies as opportunities, however, have the ability to combine these solutions with their existing assets in distinctive ways that could create new growth businesses. In June, for example, British Telecom launched a service allowing users to make phone calls over Yahoo's IM product.

Generally, incumbents to bet on are those that recognize that they need to do things differently to capitalize on emerging technologies, using new organizational forms and tolerating less-than-perfect solutions that bring new benefits to consumers.

One of the benefits of a theory-based approach is that even if you don't know precisely what will happen in the future, you can focus on the things to watch that will signal important industry changes. When an IM provider adds a feature that brings it close to the market's core, the scales tip further toward disruption. When an established telecommunications player announces plans to introduce a VoIP solution, the scales tip away from disruption.

Continually looking for signals of change, evaluating competitive battles, and watching for important strategic choices can help make sense of these kinds of developments and increase the ability to see what's next in any industry.

Reprint S0409A

About the Contributors

Scott D. Anthony is a partner at Innosight.

Clayton M. Christensen is Robert and Jane Cizik Professor of Business Administration at Harvard Business School and coauthor, with Michael E. Raynor, of *The Innovator's Solution: Creating and Sustaining Successful Growth* (Harvard Business School Press, 2003).

Gary Hamel is chairman of the Woodside Institute, a foundation whose mission is to advance organizational resilience, innovation, and renewal.

Alejandro Sayago is innovation process director for CEMEX, Mexico's cement giant.

Anthony W. Ulwick is president and CEO of Strategyn, an innovation management consultancy and enterprise software firm based in Lantana, Florida.

Loren Gary is managing editor of *Compass* magazine at the Center for Public Leadership at the John F. Kennedy School of Government, Harvard University.

Henry Chesbrough is executive director, Center for Technology Strategy and Management, Haas School of Business, University of California, Berkeley.

About the Contributors

Judith A. Ross is a Boston-based writer who frequently covers business.

Hal Plotkin is a writer and editor based in Palo Alto, California. The former editor of *Entrepreneur of the Year Magazine*, he currently writes a regular column for the San Francisco Chronicle's SFGate.com website.

Eric Mankin is the president of Innovation & Business Architectures, an advisory services firm specializing in new product and business creation.

Mark W. Johnson is president of Innosight.

Matt Eyring is managing director of Innosight.

Clare Martens is a business and IT journalist based in Waltham, Massachusetts.

Harvard Business Review Paperback Series

The Harvard Business Review Paperback Series offers the best thinking on cutting-edge management ideas from the world's leading thinkers, researchers, and managers. Designed for leaders who believe in the power of ideas to change business, these books will be useful to managers at all levels of experience, but especially senior executives and general managers. In addition, this series is widely used in training and executive development programs.

These books are priced at US$19.95
Price subject to change.

Title	Product #
Harvard Business Review **Interviews with CEOs**	3294
Harvard Business Review on **Advances in Strategy**	8032
Harvard Business Review on **Appraising Employee Performance**	7685
Harvard Business Review on **Becoming a High Performance Manager**	1296
Harvard Business Review on **Brand Management**	1445
Harvard Business Review on **Breakthrough Leadership**	8059
Harvard Business Review on **Breakthrough Thinking**	181X
Harvard Business Review on **Building Personal and Organizational Resilience**	2721
Harvard Business Review on **Business and the Environment**	2336
Harvard Business Review on **The Business Value of IT**	9121
Harvard Business Review on **Change**	8842
Harvard Business Review on **Compensation**	701X
Harvard Business Review on **Corporate Ethics**	273X
Harvard Business Review on **Corporate Governance**	2379
Harvard Business Review on **Corporate Responsibility**	2748
Harvard Business Review on **Corporate Strategy**	1429
Harvard Business Review on **Crisis Management**	2352
Harvard Business Review on **Culture and Change**	8369
Harvard Business Review on **Customer Relationship Management**	6994
Harvard Business Review on **Decision Making**	5572

To order, call 1-800-668-6780, or go online at www.HBSPress.org

Title	Product #
Harvard Business Review on **Developing Leaders**	5003
Harvard Business Review on **Doing Business in China**	6387
Harvard Business Review on **Effective Communication**	1437
Harvard Business Review on **Entrepreneurship**	9105
Harvard Business Review on **Finding and Keeping the Best People**	5564
Harvard Business Review on **Innovation**	6145
Harvard Business Review on **The Innovative Enterprise**	130X
Harvard Business Review on **Knowledge Management**	8818
Harvard Business Review on **Leadership**	8834
Harvard Business Review on **Leadership at the Top**	2756
Harvard Business Review on **Leadership in a Changed World**	5011
Harvard Business Review on **Leading in Turbulent Times**	1806
Harvard Business Review on **Managing Diversity**	7001
Harvard Business Review on **Managing High-Tech Industries**	1828
Harvard Business Review on **Managing People**	9075
Harvard Business Review on **Managing Projects**	6395
Harvard Business Review on **Managing Uncertainty**	9083
Harvard Business Review on **Managing the Value Chain**	2344
Harvard Business Review on **Managing Your Career**	1318
Harvard Business Review on **Marketing**	8040
Harvard Business Review on **Measuring Corporate Performance**	8826
Harvard Business Review on **Mergers and Acquisitions**	5556
Harvard Business Review on **Mind of the Leader**	6409
Harvard Business Review on **Motivating People**	1326
Harvard Business Review on **Negotiation**	2360
Harvard Business Review on **Nonprofits**	9091
Harvard Business Review on **Organizational Learning**	6153
Harvard Business Review on **Strategic Alliances**	1334
Harvard Business Review on **Strategies for Growth**	8850
Harvard Business Review on **Teams That Succeed**	502X
Harvard Business Review on **Turnarounds**	6366
Harvard Business Review on **What Makes a Leader**	6374
Harvard Business Review on **Work and Life Balance**	3286

Harvard Business Essentials

In the fast-paced world of business today, everyone needs a personal resource—a place to go for advice, coaching, background information, or answers. The Harvard Business Essentials series fits the bill. Concise and straightforward, these books provide highly practical advice for readers at all levels of experience. Whether you are a new manager interested in expanding your skills or an experienced executive looking to stay on top, these solution-oriented books give you the reliable tips and tools you need to improve your performance and get the job done. Harvard Business Essentials titles will quickly become your constant companions and trusted guides.

These books are priced at US$19.95, except as noted.
Price subject to change.

Title	Product #
Harvard Business Essentials: **Negotiation**	1113
Harvard Business Essentials: **Managing Creativity and Innovation**	1121
Harvard Business Essentials: **Managing Change and Transition**	8741
Harvard Business Essentials: **Hiring and Keeping the Best People**	875X
Harvard Business Essentials: **Finance for Managers**	8768
Harvard Business Essentials: **Business Communication**	113X
Harvard Business Essentials: **Manager's Toolkit ($24.95)**	2896
Harvard Business Essentials: **Managing Projects Large and Small**	3213
Harvard Business Essentials: **Creating Teams with an Edge**	290X
Harvard Business Essentials: **Entrepreneur's Toolkit**	4368
Harvard Business Essentials: **Coaching and Mentoring**	435X
Harvard Business Essentials: **Crisis Management**	4376
Harvard Business Essentials: **Time Management**	6336
Harvard Business Essentials: **Power, Influence, and Persuasion**	631X
Harvard Business Essentials: **Strategy**	6328
Harvard Business Essentials: **Decision Making**	7618
Harvard Business Essentials: **Marketer's Toolkit**	7626

How to Order

Harvard Business School Press publications are available worldwide
from your local bookseller or online retailer.
You can also call

1-800-668-6780

Our product consultants are available to help you
8:00 a.m.–6:00 p.m., Monday–Friday, Eastern Time.
Outside the U.S. and Canada, call: 617-783-7450
Please call about special discounts for quantities greater than ten.

You can order online at

www.HBSPress.org